1000+ QUESTIONS
TO ASK YOURSELF TO BECOME THE
CHAMPION
OF YOUR OWN LIFE

You Are the Hero You've Been Waiting for – Be Your Future Self Now.

The Companion / Self-Coaching Guidebook for…
Life According to The Rules of Boxing:
101 Rules to Being the Champion of Your Own Life

JOLIE GLASSMAN

BALBOA.PRESS
A DIVISION OF HAY HOUSE

Balboa Press books may be ordered through booksellers or by contacting:

Balboa Press
A Division of Hay House
1663 Liberty Drive
Bloomington, IN 47403
www.balboapress.com
844-682-1282

ISBN: 979-8-7652-3765-6 (sc)
ISBN: 979-8-7652-3766-3 (e)

Print information available on the last page.

Balboa Press rev. date: 06/09/2023

CONTENTS

Jolie Glassman is an authentic transformational leader. Some folks talk about what needs to happen, while others work diligently to make the world a better place. Working out is a real thing in all areas of life. Teaching others to become the best version of themselves is Jolie's passion. Her books compile a simple framework and best practices that can be implemented by anyone without excuses. I am fortunate to call Jolie a friend and a sister on mission to make the next generation greater than anyone could imagine. We must do better together in truth and love. Imagine heaven on earth.

-Dr. Blanca Cespedes EdD aka "Dr. C"

Academic & Career Coach
Educational Consultant & Servant Leader
Public Education Administrator

I'd like to say this is an outstanding young woman who knows the preparations required for fitness and for calculating on good health and good food. Many, many people have come to her famous gym to visit, film, celebrate and train - greats such as Muhammad Ali, Angelo Dundee, Evander Holyfield, Roy Jones Jr., Bernard Hopkins, Lennox Lewis, Chris Bosch, Will Smith, and many, many others. I offer a tribute to this woman, who is an amazing person that has transformed the lives of tens of thousands of people throughout her thirty-plus years of in-depth experience in fitness, health and wellness, business, education, transformation, inspiration, and leadership. She has her own 501(c)3 called *Jolie's Kids*, and she helps society, and the community by assisting children and families in working out and doing healthy things in this world. Jolie is the queen and the owner of this World-Famous South Beach Boxing gym. She is loved, honored, respected and admired, and I like to call her my daughter. I am so proud of her, all her hard work, and the lifelong career of experiences that went into writing this book. I know it's going to be a game changer for teens and adults, both women and men. Jolie is all about making an impact and transforming lives.

-KHALILAH CAMACHO-ALI.

former wife of Muhammad Ali, and mother to their four children together

Inspired by her passion for boxing and love of service, Jolie Glassman has written a truly inspirational book, a blueprint for anyone that is ready to fight for a better life. She uses the words and disciplines of great fighters like myself, to train and motivate the mind into obtaining characteristics that boxers use for self-mastery, which include belief, discipline, repetition, and desire. If you are ready to fight for a better life, then there's no better coach than Jolie Glassman to have in your corner.

—Mike Tyson

INTRODUCTION

Ideally, by now, you have already read my first book: *101 Rules to Being the Champion of Your Own Life* at least once, or more, and you are motivated and inspired by all the ingredients it takes to become the champion of your own life. However, you don't really know how to implement it yet and possess these qualities and skills for yourself to make it alive and real for you in your reality. *How do you truly become the hero, the champion, of your own life?* This is not a dress rehearsal, and you have one chance to live this life of yours, so make it great; or not, the choice is yours. My books are not for those who choose to *not*. My books are for those that want to become the master of their destiny, not a victim of their history. Start strong and finish strong. Try things until they become easy. Habits are the compound interest in personal development. Work harder on yourself than you do on anything else, and life will become easier. Practice good habits and get rid of bad ones. Because you die, you must live now. You are the single most important influence on your own life. Have the goal to live as long as possible while still being strong, energetic, and healthy; with satisfaction, joy, and fulfillment. How will you ever do that if you do not become fully self-reliant and the champion of your own life? One thing all of us humans were born with is the ability to choose. We choose our thoughts, behaviors, actions, beliefs, perceptions, and life paths. Between stimulus and response there's a space, and in that space lies our ability and power to choose whatever follows and comes next. Between action and reaction, there is a space. Make sure to honor that space and choose your reactions wisely. You are a choice-making individual and a meaning-making machine. Circumstances don't make us who we are; they reveal who we are. Choose wisely. Choose powerfully. Choose consciously, as you are always choosing, whether you recognize it or not, as not making a choice is also a choice. Confidence is built in the *discomfort zone*, not your comfort zone. Success equals short-term sacrifices for long-term benefits. Ask yourself, *"What are the worst things that can happen?"* Then ask yourself *"What are the best things that can happen?"* Then decide! Become a great decision-maker for yourself and your life. You are the boss of you. How does a boss think, act, behave, lead, and believe? Be the best boss ever of your own life. Govern, guide, and lead yourself accordingly to always make the next best, right choice, for yourself and your life. What does that all look like?

Fight always, from a place of love and honor yet never submit. Life is a delicate balance between intentionality and surrender. It is a balance between holding on and letting go. Gently play with the two like a slinky. You can surrender yet not submit. You can intentionally create with all the tools needed to succeed. Then give over, surrender, the rest to the Universe, God, the Higher Power that also resides in you, and all around you; *The Source* of it all. To get your way and make your dreams come true, and serve and contribute along the way; and be the torch carrier, hero, and champion of your own story, you need to possess these rules, traits, and ingredients.

Becoming the champion of your own life, and the road of success, happiness, joy, and fulfillment, all exist inside of you. You just need the right triggers and mindset to work on possessing all 101 rules. Use these as skills and traits you have working well for yourself to live as the hero you have always been waiting for. *Why wait to be who you want to be?* Be your future self now. *How does your future self behave, move, think, dress, act, etc.?* Rehearse those ways of being, now, to become and be that person. Live a created and creative life, the one you can only imagine in your wildest dreams.

With this book in your hands, you are already someone that is seeking a better and greater life. Keep going and never, ever stop. All you need to be the champion of your life is to get introspective and answer all these questions in this book for yourself. You then must take massive action while inspired. Don't wait. Life is a journey, and the destination is the journey, repeatedly, until we pass. *What is the legacy you want to leave behind? Is it a dream; or is it a goal in action to manifest and unfold over time?* Like boxers, make adversity work for you and in your favor. Boxing is a sport where the have-nots become the haves. Be like a boxer. Be triumphant over it all. You got this! Keep learning, discovering, and uncovering yourself to become the greatest, fullest, and best version of you. The pathway to get there is through curiosity, critical thinking, and massive action. My thesis for my master's was *Putting Higher Order Thinking in the Early Childhood Years.* I always say that kids turning eighteen don't pass through an archway of adulthood and acquire all it takes to operate as a success. They need to be trained and bred, to be free, critical thinkers. We don't raise children, we need to cultivate them; we raise cattle and flocks. Those who don't think outside the box are easily contained. We need to encourage their critical thinking, self-reliance, and full self-expression. In a world of information, being ignorant is a choice. Knowing isn't enough, as you need to know *how.* Our youth, and everyone, need encouragement to seek and uncover, sift and sort, and discover their best skills and talents they can offer the world while living fully self-expressed in peace, love, and happiness.

Judge by the questions asked rather than the answers given, as the true skill is in the questioning. Our lives are directly correlated to the quality of questions we ask ourselves daily. We shape our lives with the questions we ask ourselves and the answers we produce. Ask great questions and get great answers. Ask stupid, disempowering questions, and get stupid, disempowering answers. Reflect consistently on how things can be even better and then formulate even better questions to come up with the best answers. The answers for your life. Pre-think. Think critically, think smart, think period. Use your brain, challenge and question it, as everything you think is not true. All that we are is a result of what we think. If we want to be different, we need to think differently. Question your own occurring reality.

Keep what works, inspires, and empowers you. Get rid of what doesn't work, and repeat that process repeatedly. Become the master of communicating with yourself. Don't let comparison steal your joy. The biggest project you will ever work on is you, so get busy and never lose focus. When you're not focused, someone else who is will surpass you. Get a grip and interject with the self-defeating nonsense that often goes on in your head. Nobody is over there, as everywhere you go, there you are. We are meaning-making machines. Our brains just make meaning, like a coffee machine makes coffee. We are NST radio station, Non-Stop Thinking. We only need to believe and keep what works and what we want, and the rest just *let* go. Let go like cars moving by on a highway and if they stop, they crash. *So, just let that shit go.*

Have a commanding voice that honors your highest self and use it to interject when you feel like slacking or not honoring yourself. *Namaste*, is I honor the light that resides within *me*, that also resides in *you*. Just like the oxygen mask on an airplane needed for an emergency, you are directed to place the mask over your nose/mouth first, and then your small children and others. You are always first, so *be first*. Take the lead role of your own life. You are the main, primary character in your story, and everyone else is secondary. Your life is yours to lead, so be a leader; the leader of your movie, show, script, business, and life. Invest in yourself fully as the greatest investments are in yourself. Get great at being your best boss and communicating with yourself first and foremost.

Questions shape our entire thinking process. Thinking is nothing but the process of asking and answering questions. The quality of your life is the quality of the communication you have with yourself. Ask questions that empower you, inspire you, and move you into action in the desirable direction of your dreams. Notice the questions you often ask yourself that disempower you and change them to ones that empower you. You need to slow down enough to become aware of your subconscious programming. This way you can interject and reprogram your mind with what you do want rather than what you do not want. Just think of new questions that can have you discover newer, greater answers.

Don't worry, I will get you started on the road to better questioning, and here are *1,000+ Questions to Ask Yourself to Become the Champion of Your Own Life.* Each rule, ingredient, has about ten questions, some have many more, and some have fewer. They are there for you to think hard, and answer fully, whether you write it down there in the lines and spaces provided, or ponder on the question(s) throughout the day(s) in your mind. Think deeply and honestly to be able to acquire these traits and qualities, to see what you currently do, and what you currently do not possess. You will be able to take out what doesn't work, and put in what will work better. Always remember to take immediate, massive action, don't wait. You will transform your life and who you are as a person. You will dream and create your future self, and live as such *now*. Every rule is in the same order as the first book *101 Rules to Being the Champion of Your Own Life.* Start at the beginning and work your way through this workbook; the curriculum to live your life as a champion. You are more than welcome to skip around as you please and come back to ones that trigger you, or inspire you, or ones you would like to ponder and dig deeper on. My intention is for this to be a full curriculum for you to discover, uncover, create, and live your best life powerfully while being fully self-expressed and self-reliant. Time is our most precious commodity and many of our youth just sit in school and don't develop and grow into emotionally and mentally intelligent human beings. They aren't exposed and encouraged to expand themselves into their greatest selves. They are basically wasting their time in school and not getting an equal value in return for their time spent. Mental health issues are on a serious and fast rise. You need to be fit; fit in all areas, mind, body, and spirit.

Being fit is a state of readiness. Always be ready. People are learning information and facts, yet not learning coping skills and how to deal with day-to-day life, and navigating smoothly through it all. Therefore, they are frazzled and a mess, regardless of the knowledge and information they hold.

These two books are all you need to become and be, the champion of your own life. To become an anomaly you need to act like one; and in order to act like one, you need to think like one. Be curious. Be introspective. Be reflective. Evaluate and decide what is always the next best move for you, and take the daily and consistent journey to get there. To stand out from the rest and make the mark you want to leave on this planet, follow these rules. If you add other things that don't serve you and leave out things that are necessary, it is the difference in what makes a champion, or not. The first book has the famous boxers' quotes after each rule and then my breakdown of explanation, motivation, and inspiration. This workbook also has the boxers' quotes, and now in this book, every rule also includes a quote from me. Allow me to inspire you to take action in becoming the hero, the champion of your life. To follow are the questions you will ask yourself to come up with your own answers in order to possess these traits, rules, and ingredients in your life. Think deeply and be as authentic as possible. Make this your diary, your workbook, your curriculum for living a successful and powerful life you love. I recommend keeping both books together to read the rules and explanations in the first book to get inspired and creative. Then read and answer the questions in this workbook.

Let's get started. I'm so excited for you to create the life of your dreams. Discover all about yourself and show/prove to yourself how great you really are.

ABOUT ME

I come from a teaching, educational, behavioral development, leadership and entrepreneurial background. I consider myself an *MMA F.I.T. Life Coach*. I am a boxer by heart in my metaphors for life, yet like a Mixed Martial Artist, I have many tools in my toolbox of personal development, changing behavior, mindset shifting, motivating, inspiring, and magically transforming lives. I say F.I.T. as I teach you to honor yourself and *Fight for Intentional Transformation*, from a place of love, creating a win-win. I also say *FIT*, meaning a state of readiness, as I get you *fit* in mind, body, and spirit, for whatever comes your way. You become like a boxer, and bob and weave, stick and move, and flow through life. I have thirty-five plus years of total immersion in these fields by transforming people's lives on the greatest scale possible with grace and ease. I live to serve and make a difference, an impact, in every interaction. I use my skilled intentions to bring out the best in others to show them how great they are. I then hold them accountable to all they ever wanted, yet never accomplished on their own.

After being a teacher for so many years in the nineties, and owning and operating the World Famous *South Beach Boxing* since 1998, and having my *Jolie's Kids* 501©3 charity since 2016, I feel that I have come full circle to truly live out my mission of transforming the world through disrupting traditional education and teaching through my books. I generate my readers to be confident, strong, fit, healthy, happy, balanced, disciplined, self-reliant, and the champion of their own life from a very young age. The best return on my output is all the joy, satisfaction, and fulfillment I get from the results of all my clients, members, staff, and that you will now get. This proves to me I am on the right path of spreading my special sauce and sprinkling my magic on the world. I believe everyone has magic in them, and a special sauce. I like to uncover and discover that for others so they can in turn, spread their magic all over their world. I am all about results and sharing my wisdom at the precise moment needed to generate shifts and awakenings for others. My mission and drive are to make people strong, confident, self-reliant, and fit in all areas of their life, mind, body, and spirit. Now I plan to make all this happen for you as you take on your own life by answering these *1,000+ questions*. You will uncover and discover all about yourself to be the hero of your life, now.

I am so happy this book is in your hands. Self-Educate. Become self-reliant. Learn to be a humble badass. Take on your life as if it matters, as it does, as *you* matter. Become the hero of your story. Let me motivate and inspire you through my questioning to discover the best answers to getting you into massive action on creating and living your best life.

Because the questions we ask ourselves are directly correlated to the lives we create, here are some questions I often asked myself as a young child and young adult. When I was in grade school, I was terrible in physical education. I was just a terrible, slow, runner. I wasn't good in athletics and sports. I remember Mr. Sherman, my Physical Education teacher said, *Last one around the track has to run another lap.* I was so upset, and embarrassed, as I knew that person was me. I always had my outspoken mouth, so I yelled out, *That's so not fair, why would the worst person have to do it again?* In that moment, I decided, I was never going to be last again. It was not a good feeling. In life we run away from pain, even more so than we run towards pleasure. That was a painful memory for me that had me ask, *How can I finish strong and never be last again? How can I be super strong, fast, and fit?* I for sure conquered that in my life as I went on to teach in jails and detention centers; own boxing gyms, which is a male dominated sport; win Trainer of the Year Nationally in 2020; Won Best Woman in Business; Won Badass Woman in Sports, and many others. I conquered to show up far from last, and actually be the winner. I went from last in sports to Badass Woman in Sports for 2022. I fought long and hard to chase the strength in my life. I am a boxer in life. I make adversity work for me. I learned what I didn't want to have in my life, and I conquered continually to become a champion. It wasn't easy, of course, people just see the trophy and the championship belt. They don't see the hard, consistent work done day after day behind closed doors. Who we are, is who we are when no one is watching. Champions are made when no one is watching.

Then there was my home-life situation where I grew up living with my widowed mother and two older sisters. My father passed away when I was two years old, and my mom was left on her own to raise three, small children. At the time he passed, I was two, and my sisters were six and eight. My mom never got over the loss of my father. She expressed it often in her rants of rage about how she couldn't handle raising us children on her own, and keeping a roof over our heads. She would scream and yell almost daily, at the top of her lungs, about how she couldn't afford life, us, our house, and how we were going to be homeless. She remarried two times and always had a long-term boyfriend of three to five years, and there was always insane yelling and screaming. She never drank or did any drugs thankfully, and she made sure her boyfriends treated us well. They weren't the issue, she was. Watching the way she spoke to them, yelling and screaming, was the issue. She was very degrading and verbally abusive. It was not fun to be around at all. As a matter of fact, I was always on edge wondering when she was going to flip out next. I know she did the best she could, she was just not equipped, or prepared to raise us all without a father and husband. She was very strict, especially with manners, respect, and our education. We had to be straight-A students. She was extremely moody, temperamental, inconsistent, and verbally and physically abusive. Growing up in my household was not easy, yet *easy* is a word for tying our shoelaces, not for *life.* Questions I often asked myself growing up in my household were: *How do I run away, get out of my house, and get away from my mother? Who could adopt me? How do I create a life for myself independent from my mother? How do I finish school and graduate the quickest? Where do I run away to? How do I get a job so young and who will hire me while I go to school? What are my skills and the value I bring to any organization? How will I create a life to be nothing like my mother? How am I going to make it? How can I not be homeless and a nervous wreck in life?* To me growing up, I saw my mom as lazy, overweight and not a picture of what I wanted to be. I would ask myself, *How to avoid being fat? How to eat better? How to be inspired and passionate in my life? How to not need and depend on a man? How to be fully self-reliant and self-sufficient?*

We need to be careful trying so hard to not be a certain way. Balance is key, and when we resist something it persists, so oftentimes what we try not to be, we actually become. We need to accept and embrace that we all have it in us to be both ways. We need to always use our power to choose wisely and strategically from a place of love, not an ulterior reason. I needed to learn, through all my years of working on myself, to choose my mom, as she is the only mom I have. I am clear God gave me exactly what I needed to be me; and therefore, I thank and choose my mom, for all she was, and all she wasn't. She did the best she could and I came out great. As a result, I take responsibility for myself and my life, therefore I am always able to respond for my next best move to advance me in the direction of all I say I want for myself and my life.

I have my Master Practitioner License in Neuro-Linguistic Programming. In NLP, we create desirable behaviors by creating what we want and *moving toward* it, as opposed to creating what we don't want, and *moving away* from it. We learn by example and non-example. Much of my learning and decisions came from non-example, how I didn't want to be. I did many, many years of work on myself, and still do as it's an ongoing process, and includes how I viewed and interpreted my mom, my life, and my childhood. I was able to decollapse beliefs and stories I had previously collapsed, and the constraints of my past no longer constrained me. I realized my mom was far from lazy. She lived a very tough life and endured a rough childhood herself. She had many amazing qualities that I now see, focus on, and expand, as where focus goes energy flows. She passed away on my birthday in 2011, I feel she gave me life and I gave her peace. I thank God for the work I had done on myself to forgive her, and myself, and reframe the stories I had to the way things really were for the benefit of letting go and just loving her because she's my mom. I didn't have a relationship with her for most of my adult life, as I ran away at sixteen and never went back. Yet out of my participation in the Landmark Forum, a curriculum for living a powerful life, I was able to make amends with my mother and stand in my power to choose for myself and leave her with choice as well. After about six months of getting along, things were manageable. Not long after, she got all frantic and manic. I told her that if she'd like to have a relationship with me, I'd love to, but if she screams and yells at the top of her lungs whenever I call, I couldn't for my own well-being. Well, she chose to not speak to me, and she yelled frantically that she couldn't paint rainbows in the sky and pretend. Unfortunate. So, we didn't speak again 'til she passed on my birthday. I was there in the hospital to witness her with a soul and without one. It was one of the most amazing things I have ever seen in my life. When I went to visit her that day on my birthday, and I saw her soul leave the room through a slightly opened window in her hospital room, I knew she would be pronounced dead by the end of the night, as she was. Now that my mom has passed, I have lots of love, peace, and gratitude in my heart for her. We are connected in a beautiful, all knowing way where she is forgiven and appreciated, and she knows it. Sad she had to pass to get that knowing yet it's peaceful, freeing, and complete. Thank God I did the work otherwise I could have been blaming myself, and the potential for a mental health mess. We must work harder on ourselves than anything else ever in the world. I promise, life will become easier. You first. Mental health and stability are key. Prevention is easier than correction. I always say, those with good health have millions of dreams, and those without it have one.

Throughout life, up until I discovered my calling, I was sure of what I didn't want to be, yet I wasn't sure of what I did want to be. I only grew up with my mom as the adult and I didn't have much family. Therefore, I didn't have role models in the family to know what I wanted to be like, I just knew what I didn't want to be like. My role models growing up were strong women in the gyms, I thought they were so strong and beautiful. I wanted to be just like them. My other role models were the authors of the books I've read and cherished; they were my chosen role models that I sought out on my search for a better life.

Out of desperation to finish school and start a career to be fully independent and take care of myself, I found my calling. I must admit, I felt I was a bit lazy with driving to the far away campuses, so I wanted to find the most convenient way, as that would also be the quickest way for me. I went to the north campus of Florida International University, where I ended up graduating top of my class. I spoke to an advisor, and she told me about a two-year scholarship program that was entirely at the north campus. She said they accept thirty students every two years, and it is a full scholarship to a program called *F.O.C.U.S., For Our Children in Urban Settings.* I had to agree to teach two years for free while being evaluated daily in the inner cities. The program had an emphasis on Behavior Modification, as it was for alternative education and at-risk youth. I spent my entire life searching, and out of desperation, I found my inspiration. I thought it was my being lazy, as I never excelled enough in my eyes. I never believed I was good enough, yet it was out of desperation, never giving up, pushing through, and basically living out of my car for final exams, I discovered my best gifts. I was a schoolteacher and after school, I taught fitness and aerobics along with bartending on the weekends, as I was young and ambitious. I had a lot of aspirations, and I loved the freedom to do what I want when I want. I was a super hard worker.

In 1997, after I graduated from all my college, I decided to backpack around the world for six months and see all the art history and expressed religions I studied so extensively in school as Philosophy, Religion and Art History were my Minors. Upon returning, I met my ex-husband in the hottest South Beach club where I was bartending on the weekends, and he worked the front door. He was coming home from work when I was leaving to go teach school which wasn't going to be our plan together. He was going to start a business; an English Pub, a bowling alley, or a boxing gym. I heard the *gym* part and was ecstatic as that was what I was doing for many years all through college and while teaching school. I knew nothing about boxing at the time other than it was a sport of fighting, but I did know the gym business. I went on to own World Famous boxing gyms and that was the serendipity, and the beauty, of my entire life. I was always teaching *boxing*. When I was a school teacher, I would let the kids fight, one-on-one, with no one jumping in. I would clear the chairs, open the space, and allow one-on-one fighting, I just never allowed bullying. It was the key secret to banishing the bullying. It's amazing, when you teach kids to fight, they don't. Make people strong and fit, not weak and cowardly. Boxing is a gentleman's sport. If you're not humbled, it sure will make you humble. Boxing gyms, real ones, are where young kids go to save themselves. The world would be a much better place if it were more like a boxing gym.

So, over the last twenty-five plus years, I got to synergize everything I love and create an amazing life of service to others, that in turn serves me back. I am grateful and thankful for doing the work. Wisdom is not guaranteed to the aged. Wisdom comes from past experiences without emotional charges. I'm proud and pleased to be at a stage in my life where I just want to share the wisdom of my life. I was always a professional student from an early age. The best teachers are the best learners. I loved learning. I was always amazed and grateful that a teacher would stand in front of the room and just pour knowledge into me. I was always inquisitive and wanted to know more. The great thing about my mom, because she was never around since she made chocolate novelties through the night and slept much of the morning to early afternoon. She was still very strict with manners and education, yet she gave us the freedom to learn all about the various religions and history, so we lived in the libraries. She encouraged us to be critical, free thinkers, and we were all three honor students and always at the top of our class. I have read well over seven hundred books for the sole purpose of personal and self-development. Those authors and books were my role models. I would follow the authors on their book tours all over since the eighties. I would go attend their seminars and workshops, I would watch them speak, and I had all the cassette tapes for everything I could ever need to be successful. I would listen always and would seek to be better and better. After all, I always wanted to get out of my house quickly and to be nothing like my mom. I wanted to be independent, self-sufficient, successful, strong, and happy. I wanted to live joyfully and have total freedom of my life's choices. I always wanted to be better and sought out whatever that meant for the present moment. The questions I asked myself shaped my life, as yours do as well.

Just when you think you got it all figured out and you got a handle on everything, life throws more problems and curve balls your way. I've bobbed and weaved, did the internal work, and came out stronger each time. I went through a terrible and nasty, in the public eye, long divorce in 2008; ran my gyms through several economic crashes and a pandemic shut down; and had a terrible motorcycle accident in 2012 that left me on a journey of recovery, self-discovery, and self-reliant wellness for my path. The only people without problems are dead, so don't see them as problems, see them as opportunities for growth, because they are. Being a human means being a fighter. We all fight. We fight for the things we believe in; we also fight for those we love. At times we must fight against our greatest opponent, ourselves. Be the champion fighter of your life. Win. Succeed. The more tools you have in your toolbox to manage all that life throws at you, the better equipped you are to be fit, balanced, ready, prepared, and successful.

We need to stand guard at the gate of our minds, and not let just anything in, other than what we choose. Mindset is everything. *Who are your role models and teachers? What is going into your brain, and from what sources?* We program our brains like computer programmers; garbage in, garbage out. Everything we think, say, and do is a choice. Slow down enough to notice. Good thoughts produce good habits, and bad thoughts produce bad habits. Begin choosing instead of excusing. Stop believing you're a victim of your genetic makeup, as your beliefs can change your genes. It's the environment that signals your genes, not your genes that signals the environment. If our thoughts can make us sick, then our thoughts can also make us well. Make yourself healthy and well with your thoughts. You are what you believe yourself to be, so believe in yourself, and become all you aspire to be. Only you have the power to make it happen. You are in charge, so take charge.

Demand of yourself excellent performance and results. If you want an extraordinary life and results, you need to be extraordinary and do extraordinary things. Perform year after year as diamonds are made under pressure. Withstand the pressure and get comfortable with being uncomfortable, until being uncomfortable is comfortable. I can inspire and share with you, but you must demand it of yourself and act accordingly. If you want your life to change, then you need to change. If you want your life to get better, then you need to get better.

Consistent and constant improvement is where the magic happens. Then contribute and serve along the way to live in joy and fulfillment. Receiving is reserved for the giving, so start the giving process and you will receive back ten-fold.

Don't seek abundance, generate it. Don't seek freedom, generate it. If you love life, it will love you back, as whatever you put out in the world comes right back to you. Everything is energy and vibration. Generate great energy and align to the vibrational frequencies you want to exist. People who make the best out of life get the best out of it. Things turn out best for those who make the best of how things turn out. What matters is what you do with what you have.

Keep your thoughts positive because they become your words and then your behaviors. Then your behaviors become your habits and then it becomes what you value. It all starts with you and your thoughts. Words cast spellings, so choose your thoughts and words wisely and manifest consciously. You don't have to see the whole staircase to take the next step. Just take the next step, be consistent, and climb that staircase to success. Change your questions, change your life. Ask yourself, *What is it that I truly want? What are the results I'm looking to achieve? What have I been doing to get there? What do I need to be doing and with what frequency? What do I need to stop doing? How do I need to behave?* Clarity is power. When you get better, everything will get better. Don't worry so much about how you will do it, just know where you want to go, stay in action, and the Universe will hook you up. The answers will come. Welcome to the journey.

I am your tow truck when you get stuck in the mud of life. You can lead a horse to water.....it's my job to make you thirsty.

Allow the questions in this book to ignite the thirst and hunger in you to take your life to a whole new level as the hero and champion you are of your own life story.

ACKNOWLEDGEMENTS

I'd like to acknowledge and thank all my teachers, as I myself am a teacher now carrying the torch with my unique flare, yet backed and developed by phenomenal teachers and thought leaders of the past and present. I would also like to thank all my family, friends, staff, gym members, and clients as they all brought me joy and fulfillment. They have filled me back up in return with the lives they lead, impact, and serve. Also all the boxers in the world that train like champions and live the *hero's journey* as boxers are my inspiration and metaphor for my teachings. I also want to acknowledge and thank *you* for getting this self-coaching guide book and taking on your life with consistent, next-best actions, passion, love, and igniting the spark that is already within you to shine at its brightest and light up your world and the world around you. *Thank You, and Namaste.*

Words from Rocky Balboa:

"Let me tell you something you already know. The world ain't all sunshine and rainbows. It is a very mean and nasty place and it will beat you to your knees and keep you there permanently if you let it. You, me, or nobody is gonna hit as hard as life. But it ain't how hard you hit; it's about how hard you can get hit, and keep moving forward. How much can you take, and keep moving forward? That's how winning is done. Now, if you know what you're worth, then go out and get what you're worth. But you gotta be willing to take the hit, and not pointing fingers saying you ain't where you are because of him, or her, or anybody. Cowards do that and that ain't you. You're better than that!"

#1

ALWAYS CHASE THE PERFECT PUNCH

I fight for perfection. Never achieve it, no one does, but we aim for it.
-Mike Tyson

*No matter how much you work on perfecting your craft, there
is always more to get to, another level to achieve. You never get
there, as the destination is the journey, and you never fully master
a craft, as you are always chasing that perfect punch.*
-Jolie Glassman

1. What is an area of your life that you're working on perfecting your craft?

   _____

   _____

   _____

   _____

   _____

2. How's it going? What are you doing that is working, and what is not working?

   _____

   _____

   _____

   _____

   _____

3. Is there anything you'd like to add to become even better? What? List them.

   _____

   _____

   _____

   _____

   _____

4. Are there any distractions or activities you can take out, that hold you back from progressing? What? List them.

_____

_____

_____

_____

_____

_____

5. Are there other activities or endeavors you'd like to learn, and study? What are they?

_____

_____

_____

_____

_____

6. In what area of your life, can you work harder/smarter, to reach a higher level of mastery?

_____

_____

_____

_____

_____

7. What actions can you take and implement, that will propel you forward, in the desirable direction?

_____

_____

_____

_____

_____

8. Who do you need to reach out to?

_____

_____

_____

_____

_____

9. By when will you do it?

_____

_____

_____

_____

_____

#2

WHEREVER YOU GO, THERE YOU ARE

To see a man beaten not by a better opponent but by himself is a tragedy.
-Cus D'Amato

Nobody is over there. It is always you, your thoughts,
perceptions, beliefs, values, and stories. Everywhere you go
there you are. We're all in our own World, in one World.
-Jolie Glassman

1. What's an area of your life that could use a different spin or view on the story that you gave it?

   _____
   _____
   _____
   _____
   _____

2. What are some different views or stories you can give it? Get creative.

   _____
   _____
   _____
   _____
   _____

3. Who are you being, and showing up as, in your stories? Is it who you need to be? If not, who do you need to be? What do you need to do differently?

   _____
   _____
   _____
   _____

4. List ten of your strongest beliefs.

_____

_____

_____

_____

_____

5. Think of other possible viewpoints to each belief that can also be true. Write them down.

_____

_____

_____

_____

_____

6. Are any of your beliefs not serving you? Which ones can you think of? Think of your *limiting* beliefs. Write them down.

_____

_____

_____

_____

_____

7. What are some empowering statements, beliefs, you can think about and practice, instead?

_____

_____

_____

_____

_____

8. Say those empowering statements in the mirror 10x and reflect on how it went.

_____

_____

_____

_____

_____

9. Which ones resonate with you most, and make you feel great?

_____

_____

_____

_____

_____

- *Make those your mantras. BE THOSE.*

#3

BELIEVE IN YOURSELF-
CONFIDENCE IS KEY

Confidence breeds success and success breed confidence.
Confidence applied properly surpasses genius.
-Mike Tyson

To be a champ, you have to believe in yourself when no one else will.
-Sugar Ray Leonard

*You can't win without confidence. If my mind can conceive
it, if my heart can believe it - then I can achieve it.*
-Muhammad Ali

*Have a strong command voice that empowers you to honor yourself and take action.
Say what you want to believe and do what it takes to manifest that belief.
You need self-belief to chase your own greatness.*
-Jolie Glassman

1. What are the conversations you have with yourself that you no longer want to have?

_____

_____

_____

_____

2. Which conversations would you rather have?

_____

_____

_____

_____

3. Do you feel you are a person who believes in yourself and has a great amount of confidence? Explain your answer and why you feel this way.

_____

_____

_____

_____

4. What are your strengths and areas you feel most confident?

_____

_____

_____

_____

5. Where do you feel the least confident? What are things you can say to yourself instead that can make you feel better and move you into a positive, forward moving direction?

_____

_____

_____

_____

6. What actions will you need to take to feel more confident? By when will you take them?

_____

_____

_____

_____

7. Practice/rehearse the empowering conversations you would rather have, and get into that state of being. Practice feeling that way. Do this work in the mirror. Journal the results, below.

_____

_____

_____

_____

8. What can you do to take better care of yourself physically, mentally, and emotionally?

_____

_____

_____

_____

9. What is the worst that could happen if you fail, and how can you prepare for that outcome?

_____

_____

_____

_____

#4

DEVELOP THE INTERNAL IMMUNITY OF GRIT

There are three things you need to remember in boxing,
work hard, work harder, work hardest.
-Manny Pacquiao

Grit is the driver of achievement and success. It is a mixture of
courage, perseverance, and resilience in the face of setbacks.
Grit requires passion, consistency, and the ability to learn from criticism.
Developing the internal immunity of grit builds character.
-Jolie Glassman

1. What is an area of your life where you possess a lot of grit, and why do you think this is?

    _____
    _____
    _____
    _____
    _____
    _____
    _____
    _____
    _____

2. Where is grit needed that is missing in your life?

    _____
    _____
    _____
    _____
    _____
    _____
    _____
    _____

3. Which ingredients are you missing?

_____

_____

_____

_____

_____

_____

4. Which skills do you need to gain?

_____

_____

_____

_____

_____

5. In which area do you want to tackle, and develop more grit?

_____

_____

_____

_____

_____

_____

6. What will you do specifically, and by when, to demonstrate growth in grit?

_____

_____

_____

_____

_____

_____

7. How will you feel while demonstrating?

_____

_____

_____

_____

_____

_____

Meditate with the vision and those feelings, now. Make your internal experiences stronger than any other experiences, then follow the rules and allow all you have dreamed and imagined to come true.

#5
WILLINGNESS TO SACRIFICE

I'm willing to do anything to myself to improve to be the best. I'm willing to sacrifice my body, my psychological health, to just be the best in the world. That's what sacrifice is, you really have to sacrifice your life. I do what others are not willing to do. When you have something in life that you want to accomplish greatly, you have to be willing to give up your happiness.
-Mike Tyson

Chasing mastery; becoming a champion; competing with the big dogs; being the hero of your own life; looking back without regret; and obtaining a feeling of success, fulfillment, and satisfaction all require a willingness to sacrifice.
-Jolie Glassman

1. In which area of your life do you sacrifice the most and why is that the case?

_____

_____

_____

2. What does sacrifice look like for you? What is your process and how does it make you feel?

_____

_____

_____

3. What results are you sacrificing for?

_____

_____

_____

4. What do you lose, and what do you gain, by sacrificing all you do?

_____
_____
_____

5. Has it been worth the sacrifice? Why or why not?

_____
_____
_____

6. In which area of your life do you need to sacrifice more in order to get the desirable results?

_____
_____
_____

7. What is holding you back?

_____
_____
_____

8. How badly do you want the results and what are you willing to do to ensure you get them?

_____
_____
_____

9. What behaviors and attitudes do you need to exemplify in order to sacrifice what you need to get where and what you want?

_____
_____
_____

10. What specific actions can and will you take, to get the results you want?

_____
_____
_____

11. In the areas you sacrifice to get what you want, how do you get through the sacrifice. How does it make you feel, once accomplished, knowing you sacrificed so much to get there?

_____
_____
_____

- *Practice feeling those ways more often. When tackling something that requires sacrifice, trigger yourself into feeling accomplished and do what it takes to get there while existing in these feelings.*

#6

BOB AND WEAVE, STICK AND MOVE

Life doesn't run away from nobody. Life runs at people.
-Joe Frazier

You either run the day, or the day runs you. Do not get hit head-on or smacked in the face; rather, anticipate, see it coming, and then bob and weave, and stick and move.
-Jolie Glassman

1. Where in life do you feel you keep getting knocked down?

   _____

   _____

   _____

   _____

   _____

2. Who are you being, and what are you feeling, in those moments?

   _____

   _____

   _____

   _____

   _____

3. What can you do and feel instead?

   _____

   _____

   _____

   _____

4. Where in life do you feel you bob and weave successfully?

_____
_____
_____
_____
_____

5. Who are you being in these situations and how do you feel?

_____
_____
_____
_____
_____

6. What can you apply, feelings or actions, to smoothly get through situations where you keep getting smacked and knocked down?

_____
_____
_____
_____
_____

7. Who can support and assist you?

_____
_____
_____
_____
_____

8. What activities or practices can calm you down and ground yourself to better focus on the areas you feel defeated?

_____
_____
_____
_____
_____

9. What can you implement in future situations to proactively anticipate, so you don't get pummeled?

_____
_____
_____
_____
_____

#7

OWN YOUR POWER

*Promoters need you. You don't need them, the boxer has
the leverage, and a lot of boxers don't know that.*
-Ryan Garcia

*Through self-talk, self-discipline, and movement, you must intervene with
yourself and empower yourself. Take charge and be the boss of you!
Know your power, and then own your power.*
-Jolie Glassman

1. Do you find it difficult to speak up about what matters most to you? Why, or why not, do you think that is?

   _____

   _____

   _____

   _____

   _____

2. What feelings arise when it's time for you to speak up and express yourself?

   _____

   _____

   _____

   _____

3. Discover the language that empowers you. Write it down here. Think! Inspire yourself with your language. What are those words and phrases?

   _____

   _____

   _____

   _____

4. Which activities make you feel the most empowered?

_____
_____
_____
_____
_____
_____

5. Which areas of life are you not fully self-expressed, and you don't speak up and honor yourself and own your power, and why do you think that is?

_____
_____
_____
_____
_____
_____

6. What are you saying to yourself in those areas?

_____
_____
_____
_____
_____

7. What actions are you taking in those areas?

_____
_____
_____
_____
_____

8. What can you be, say, and do, differently to feel empowered?

_____
_____
_____
_____
_____

9. How will you implement these things and at what moments? What will you rehearse?

_____
_____
_____
_____
_____

#8

THE FOUNDATION AND BASICS ARE EVERYTHING

People have just said about me so far that I'm just a big puncher,
but I showed that I can command a fight behind my jab,
which is the foundation of all good boxing.
-Daniel Dubois

It's very important to constantly practice the basics and work at
getting better at them, as they create what comes from them, and
what comes after them. The basics and foundation need
to be on point for anything that follows them to work.
-Jolie Glassman

1. Where in life is your foundation slacking? Your relationships? Career? Business? Personal life? Health? Spirituality?

_____

_____

_____

_____

_____

2. What exactly is missing?

_____

_____

_____

_____

_____

_____

_____

3. Can it be rectified? Can you accomplish it yourself, or do you need assistance?

_____
_____
_____
_____
_____
_____

4. What happened in the beginning that the foundation is not solid?

_____
_____
_____
_____
_____
_____

5. Where in life is your foundation great, you are smooth sailing, and you know what you are doing?

_____
_____
_____
_____
_____

6. Why do you think that is?

_____
_____
_____
_____
_____

7. Who are you being in these areas and what have you done differently?

_____
_____
_____
_____
_____

8. Can you apply anything to the areas that are slacking? What?

_____
_____
_____
_____
_____

#9
COMMITMENT TO EXCELLENCE

Don't you understand anything about commitment, about being a pro, about sticking with what you say you wanna be? You don't just say it when you feel good. You don't just say it when you're not tired. You don't do it just when it's sunny. You do it everyday of your life. You do it when it hurts to do it, when it's the last thing in the world you wanna do, when there are a million reasons not to do it. You do it because you're a professional.
-Teddy Atlas

I am gonna show you how great I am.
-Muhammad Ali

When you are excellent, you become unforgettable, and that is what we all want. Commit to being excellent. Do the right things. It will always bring the right things to you. Grow yourself into the best of yourself. I am gonna show you how great you are.
-Jolie Glassman

1. What are you committed to doing, and what results are you committed to achieving?

_____

_____

_____

2. Does it show consistent commitment in your results? Can you be/do more?

_____

_____

_____

_____

3. What's missing that you can add, to get better results?

_____
_____
_____
_____
_____
_____

4. Who are you committed to being?

_____
_____
_____
_____
_____
_____

5. What are you excellent at and who are you being when you are excellent?

_____
_____
_____
_____
_____
_____

6. What is your (greatest) expression in the world?

_____
_____
_____
_____
_____

7. Where are you slacking in your commitments? Why?

_____
_____
_____
_____
_____

8. What is missing to have them come to fruition?

_____
_____
_____
_____
_____

#10
KNOW YOURSELF

The whole key is to be honest with yourself, find the weak spots, work on it, get it done.
-Wladimir Klitschko

My wealth is in my knowledge of self, love and spirituality.
-Muhammad Ali

You are limitless and endless and possess everything you need inside yourself. Dive in deep, become your own best friend, and get to know yourself. We are the universe's parts that get to know themselves better. Listen. The quieter you become, the more you can hear.
-Jolie Glassman

1. What are things you like about yourself?
    _____
    _____
    _____
    _____

2. What are things you like to do?
    _____
    _____
    _____
    _____

3. What do you feel are your greatest strengths?
    _____
    _____
    _____
    _____

4. What area(s) would you like to work on becoming greater?

_____

_____

_____

_____

5. Do you know yourself well? Why or why not? In which ways?

_____

_____

_____

_____

6. What is an area of your life that's not working as well as you'd like it to? Explain what's not working.

_____

_____

_____

_____

7. What are the thoughts you have about yourself in that area?

_____

_____

_____

_____

8. What needs to happen, who do you need to be, and what do you need to think to have that work for you?

_____

_____

_____

9. Where do you need to go to understand yourself better?

_____

_____

_____

10. How will you go down that path, and gain a deeper understanding of yourself; so you can recognize, become aware, and choose powerfully to not have it constrain you anymore?

_____

_____

_____

11. Will you need support? A coach? An accountability partner? Who?

_____

_____

_____

#11
BE STRATEGIC

In boxing you create a strategy to beat each new opponent, it's just like chess.

-Lennox Lewis

I love to always create a win-win situation.

In communicating, I am strategic in my word choice so that it serves me, and then serves and honors the other person and what it is I'm wanting to accomplish in the interaction.

Be strategic in all endeavors.

-Jolie Glassman

1. Do you consider yourself a strategic person? Why or why not? In what ways?

_____

_____

_____

_____

2. In which area(s) could you be more strategic?

_____

_____

3. What can you do to further enhance the strategy? What skills and knowledge do you need to acquire?

_____

_____

_____

_____

4. Which area(s) do you consider yourself very strategic?

5. What is great about you, that has you so strategic in that area? How do you think and behave? What do you do?

6. What can be applied to an area you need to be strategic in, that you do here, and don't do in that area?

7. What do you do in your life, your work, and your communications that involves strategy?

8. Do you feel you strategize before you attack most endeavors? How? In what ways?

9. How does your ability to strategize play a role in your success?

10. What can you do, and who can you become, to strategize in more areas?

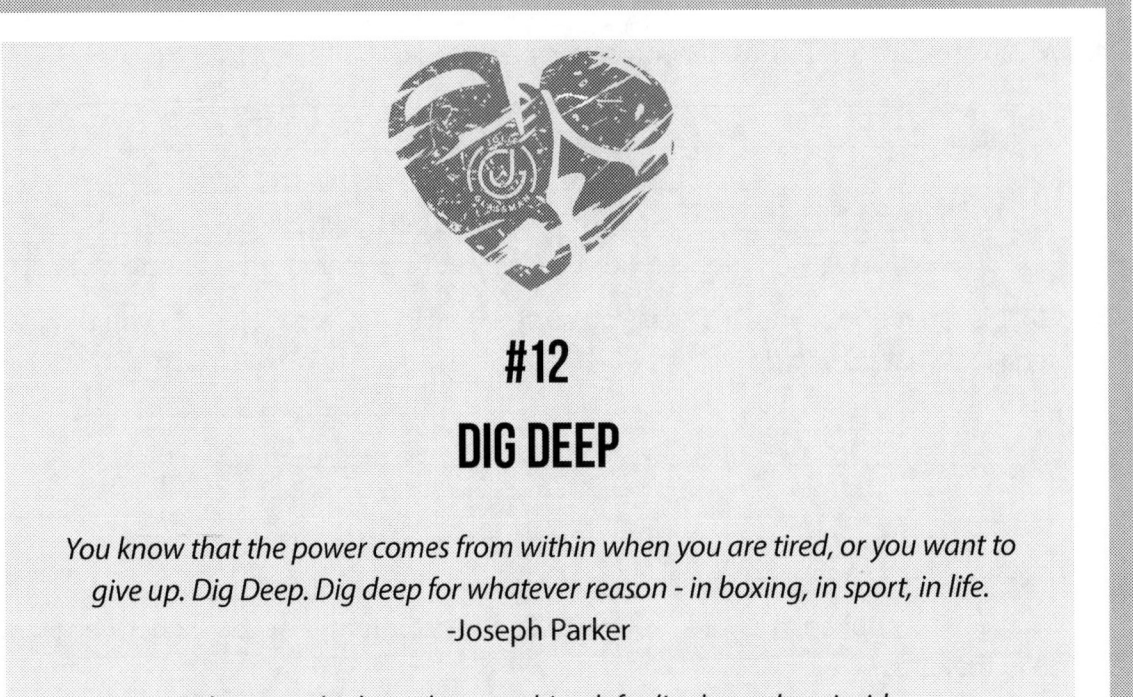

#12

DIG DEEP

You know that the power comes from within when you are tired, or you want to give up. Dig Deep. Dig deep for whatever reason - in boxing, in sport, in life.
-Joseph Parker

When you think you have nothing left, dig down deep inside and give it more. Make being strong your only choice.
-Jolie Glassman

1. Which area(s) of your life could use more effort?

   _____
   _____
   _____
   _____

2. What holds you back from giving your maximum effort in these areas? What happens?

   _____
   _____
   _____
   _____

3. What actions can you take to accomplish what you want?

   _____
   _____
   _____
   _____

4. Who do you need to be, and become, to accomplish more and dig deeper?

   _____
   _____
   _____

5. Where do you feel you're doing great and you *dig deep*? Why is that?

_____

_____

_____

_____

_____

6. How else can you move the needle forward to be even greater?

_____

_____

_____

_____

_____

7. Do you dig deep when necessary? Explain.

_____

_____

_____

_____

_____

8. What holds you back?

_____

_____

_____

_____

_____

9. How can you get out of your own way, and not hold yourself back, and in which areas?

_____

_____

_____

_____

10. Are you willing to do what it takes? What will this look like for you in your life?

_____

_____

_____

_____

11. By when, and with what frequency, will you start implementing?

_____

_____

_____

_____

#13

FIGHT, THINK, LEARN, AND BE SMART

I'm on the record for five losses or something like that, but the one guy who really whipped me was Muhammad Ali. And it taught me one big lesson. That no matter how big and strong you are, you're going to have to use your mind. You must think things out.
-George Foreman

You have good days, you have bad days. But the main thing is to grow mentally.
-Floyd Mayweather Jr.

Everybody thinks this is a tough man's sport. This is not a tough man's sport. This is a thinking man's sport. A tough man is gonna get hurt real bad in this sport.
-Mike Tyson

Turn your woes into wisdom. Wisdom is your knowledge gained from past experiences without an emotional charge. Learn. Know better. Do better. Be wise.
-Jolie Glassman

1. Which areas in your life do you think hard and smart to get great results?

_____

_____

_____

_____

2. Who are you being in those areas where you are strong, smart and get great results?

_____

_____

_____

_____

3. Which area of your life do you need to know more and be stronger?

_____

_____

_____

_____

_____

_____

4. What will you do, and what courses will you take, to get this knowledge and grow?

_____

_____

_____

_____

_____

_____

_____

5. Do you challenge your brain?

_____

_____

_____

_____

_____

_____

_____

6. How do you challenge your brain?

_____

_____

_____

_____

_____

_____

7. What else can you do, that you would love to do, to challenge your brain and grow?

_____

_____

_____

_____

_____

_____

_____

#14

DON'T BE A FOLLOWER

I never was a person that wanted that life. I'm a leader not a follower. I don't care what they say, or what they're doing or what they're wearing. Go ahead, cos come Judgment Day, all of that won't matter. How many people did you help? How many people did you talk to? How many people did you try to encourage? How many people did you bring to God? That's what's gon' matter.
-Roy Jones Jr.

Don't follow the crowd; let them follow you.
-George Foreman

We need a social media platform of leaders supporting leaders, not followers. Everyone can be a leader, and we need them to be. Lead by example. Be the change. If the people lead, the leaders will follow.
-Jolie Glassman

1. Where are you a leader in life? In which areas?

_____

_____

_____

_____

_____

2. Which qualities do you exemplify and possess that make you a leader in these areas?

_____

_____

_____

_____

_____

3. What results do you have that show your leadership?

_____

_____

_____

_____

4. Which area in your life do you need to lead more effectively?

_____

_____

_____

5. What can you do differently?

_____

_____

_____

6. What stops you from leading and being fully self-expressed?

_____

_____

_____

7. Do you consider yourself a leader? Why or why not?

_____

_____

_____

8. Which traits and qualities are missing that would make you more of a leader?

_____

_____

_____

9. How do leaders walk, act, behave?

_____

_____

_____

10. How do you walk, act, behave?

_____

_____

_____

11. How do you need to walk, act, behave?

_____

_____

_____

#15

NEVER THE SAME TIMING, RHYTHM, OR TEMPO

Rhythm is everything in boxing. Every move you make starts with your heart, and that's in rhythm or you're in trouble.
-Sugar Ray Robinson

Moments between the notes create the music. Never use the same timing, rhythm, or tempo. Music is made up as much of silence as it is out of sound. Honor the space; it is needed. Create space; it is needed.
-Jolie Glassman

1. Do you meditate? If so, for how long, and how often? I recommend meditating 2x a day, morning and night.

_____

_____

_____

_____

_____

_____

_____

2. Do you connect to your heart? When you get upset, do you know how to control your state of being and your temperament? Why or why not? If so, how do you do it?

_____

_____

_____

_____

_____

_____

_____

3. Do you take time and space to refill your own cup and recover? How?

_____
_____
_____
_____
_____
_____
_____
_____
_____

4. Do you journal and reserve time to think and imagine your life, and a created future? When? How often?

_____
_____
_____
_____
_____
_____
_____
_____
_____

5. Write down ten things you would like to create for yourself and your future.
    Just take twenty to thirty minutes to breathe, imagine, and relax into these visions. See them clearly with enthusiasm, joy, and gratitude.

_____
_____
_____
_____
_____
_____
_____
_____
_____

6. Write down how you can smoothly incorporate these things into your life?

_____
_____
_____
_____
_____
_____
_____
_____
_____

#16
TRAIN TO WIN

The fight is won or lost far away from witnesses - behind the lines, in the gym, and out there on the road, long before I dance under those lights.
-Muhammad Ali

Know what you want out of a situation and go after it obsessively. Feel your win. See your win. Imagine your win. Savor your win, and chase whom you need to become to accomplish the win.
-Jolie Glassman

1. Do you have a winning mindset? Explain your response.

_____
_____
_____
_____
_____

2. Which characteristic/traits do you possess that create winning results?

_____
_____
_____
_____
_____

3. Which characteristics do you need to obtain and embody, to get better results?

_____
_____
_____
_____
_____

4. What will you do to possess them?

_____
_____
_____
_____
_____
_____
_____

5. What are you currently hungry for winning?

_____
_____
_____
_____
_____
_____
_____

6. Are you taking all necessary steps to accomplish it?

_____
_____
_____
_____
_____
_____
_____

7. What's missing?

_____
_____
_____
_____
_____
_____

8. By when will you add these things and with what frequency?

_____
_____
_____
_____
_____
_____

#17

BE INTENTIONAL

You have to know you can win. You have to think you can win.
You have to feel you can win.
-Sugar Ray Leonard

Intention is not something to do; it is something to connect to and align with
to create desired outcomes.
-Jolie Glassman

1. What are things you do with great intention?

    _____
    _____
    _____
    _____
    _____
    _____

2. How do you feel when doing those things and who are you being?

    _____
    _____
    _____
    _____
    _____

3. Are there things you do without intention? How often?

    _____
    _____
    _____
    _____
    _____

4. What are those things?

_____
_____
_____
_____
_____

5. How do you feel doing those things?

_____
_____
_____
_____
_____

6. Compare the things you do with and without intention. What's the difference?

_____
_____
_____
_____

7. What do you surmise and gather? How do you feel in the different scenarios?

_____
_____
_____
_____
_____

8. In which areas do you need to be more intentional?

_____
_____
_____
_____

9. Who are you being when you are not intentional?

_____
_____
_____
_____

10. How will you become more intentional in these areas? What will you do, and with what frequency?

_____
_____
_____
_____

#18

SEE EVERYTHING

The punch that knocks a man out is the punch that he didn't see.
-Cus D'Amato

The hand can't hit what the eye can't see.
-Muhammad Ali

You need convergent focus and divergent focus. You need to see a close-up and an expanded, even disassociated, view all at the same time. See it all. Notice what is all around you and right in front of your face.
-Jolie Glassman

1. Do you feel that you are a perceptive person and you sense/feel things prior to its occurrence?

_____

_____

_____

_____

_____

_____

_____

2. Why did you answer the way you did? What makes you perceptive? In what ways?

_____

_____

_____

_____

_____

_____

3. Where/when have you been blindsided before?

_____

4. What happened?

_____

5. What could have prevented you from being blindsided?

_____

6. Which skills do you possess that assist you in being more perceptive?

_____

7. What support, or assistance, can you add to be able to notice, become aware, and perceive more?

_____

#19

PRACTICE IS KEY AND YOU CAN NEVER PRACTICE ENOUGH

*There are always improvements to make, no boxer
in the world does everything right.*
-Luke Campbell

*Mastery comes from repetition. When you are rewarded in public, you are
actually being rewarded for what you practice in private. Repetition is the
mother of all mastery. Champions are made when no one is watching.*
-Jolie Glassman

1. Which areas do you excel?

   _____
   _____
   _____
   _____
   _____

2. Which attributes made you excel in these areas?

   _____
   _____
   _____
   _____

3. What is your profession, or what do you want your profession to be?

   _____
   _____
   _____
   _____

4. What do you practice consistently to get better?

_____
_____
_____
_____
_____

5. What do you need to practice more to become better?

_____
_____
_____
_____
_____

6. What is holding you back from getting better and practicing more consistently?

_____
_____
_____
_____
_____

7. How will you implement more practice?

_____
_____
_____
_____
_____

8. When will you do it by?

_____
_____
_____
_____

9. What will your consistent schedule of more practicing look like?

_____
_____
_____
_____

10. What else do you want to practice more of to gain more knowledge and expertise in?

_____
_____
_____
_____

#20

BE RESILIENT

A setback only paves the way for a comeback.
-Evander Holyfield

I got knocked down. Anybody could be knocked down, anybody can be knocked out, but it's not what happened, but what happens next."
-Bernard Hopkins

If you never know failure, you will never know success.
-Sugar Ray Leonard

Our circumstances do not make us who we are; they reveal who we are.
So, take the hit and come back stronger.
It is always about the comeback and never about the setback.
-Jolie Glassman

1. Are you a person that exemplifies resilience? Why or why not?

    _____
    _____
    _____
    _____
    _____

2. What are some of the great struggles you have faced in life?

    _____
    _____
    _____
    _____
    _____

3. Do you feel you come back stronger? Explain.

_____
_____
_____
_____
_____
_____
_____
_____

4. What prevents you from succeeding when you have a setback?

_____
_____
_____
_____
_____
_____
_____
_____
_____

5. How can you diminish the time it takes for you to come back stronger?

_____
_____
_____
_____
_____
_____
_____
_____

6. Which emotions do you need to feel? Which phrases would you want to say to yourself?

_____
_____
_____
_____
_____
_____
_____

#21

FACE YOUR FEARS HEAD-ON

Fear is like fire; it can be helpful if you know how to use it.
If not, you'll get burned.
-Mike Tyson

The hero and the coward both feel the same thing. But the hero uses his fear,
projects it onto his opponent, while the coward runs. It's the same thing,
fear, but it's what you do with it that matters.
-Cus D'Amato

Fear is imagination undirected. Faith is imagination directed.
So face your fears and have faith.
-Jolie Glassman

1. Are you a person who faces your fears head-on? Explain.

_____
_____
_____
_____
_____
_____

2. How many of your greatest fears actually ever happened? Explain.

_____
_____
_____
_____
_____
_____

3. What are your fears?

_____
_____
_____
_____
_____
_____
_____

4. Which fears stop you from moving forward with endeavors in your life?

_____
_____
_____
_____
_____
_____
_____

5. Can you move through and handle them?

_____
_____
_____
_____
_____
_____
_____

6. How will you face your fears, and move through them?

_____
_____
_____
_____
_____

7. Do you need support? An accountability partner? State your needs, how and when you plan to fulfill them.

_____
_____
_____
_____
_____
_____

#22

BELIEVE IT,
THEN YOU WILL SEE IT

*It's the repetition of affirmations that leads to belief. And once that
belief becomes a deep conviction, things begin to happen.*
-Muhammad Ali

I am the greatest, I said that even before I knew I was.
-Muhammad Ali

*Choose your thoughts the way you want them to manifest. You need to first
believe it, and then you can see it manifest for yourself and your life.*
-Jolie Glassman

1. What are some of the beliefs that work for you and your life? Write at least eight.

_____

_____

_____

_____

_____

_____

2. What are some limiting beliefs in your views of the World? Write at least eight.

_____

_____

_____

_____

_____

_____

3. What are some of the limiting beliefs you have about yourself? List at least eight.

_____
_____
_____
_____
_____
_____
_____
_____
_____
_____
_____
_____

4. What can you specifically say instead, to turn your limiting beliefs into empowering ones? Think hard and reframe your beliefs. Choose the best, most empowering ones, and practice them often throughout your day as affirmations.

_____
_____
_____
_____
_____
_____
_____
_____
_____
_____
_____

5. Write at least five things down that you want for yourself and your future life. Write them as if you have them now, and are grateful for their arrival and presence in your life. *Believe it, then you will see it.*

_____
_____
_____
_____
_____
_____
_____
_____
_____
_____

#23

ADJUST AND RESPOND
BEST UNDER PRESSURE

Tough times don't last, tough people do.
-Floyd Mayweather Jr.

We are all controlled by our states. The best skill set is to be able to quickly change your state to a conducive, more desirable state.
-Jolie Glassman

1. How do you feel you perform under pressure? Describe how you behave.

_____
_____
_____
_____
_____

2. Explain your answer and if you're pleased with the way you perform, or if you'd like to perform differently, and if so, how?

_____
_____
_____
_____
_____

3. Which areas are you not performing as well as you'd like to perform?

_____
_____
_____
_____

4. What is missing?

_____

_____

_____

_____

_____

5. When you do perform at your best, what are some of the things you say to yourself?

_____

_____

_____

_____

_____

6. When you don't perform as well, what are the things you say? *Notice. Become aware. Self-correct accordingly.*

_____

_____

_____

_____

_____

7. What are some things that you want to say when you perform at your best? What do you want to say when your performance is not up to par, and for what reasons? List at least two each and explain.

_____

_____

_____

_____

_____

8. Pressure is what creates diamonds. What are some amazing things you have done and/ or created when under the most pressure? List at least 3 events.

_____

_____

_____

_____

9. Explain why you perform under pressure. How can you behave as if the pressure was on, even though it's not, to produce diamond-like results?

_____

_____

_____

_____

#24

NO ONE IS COMING TO SAVE YOU

Once the bell rings you're on your own. It's just you and the other guy.
-Joe Louis

You are born alone, you die alone, and you are never alone.
-Jolie Glassman

1. Where do you feel super strong and empowered? List at least five areas/things.

_____
_____
_____
_____
_____

2. Why do you feel you are strong and empowered in those areas/things? Explain.

_____
_____
_____
_____

3. In which areas do you feel unsafe and alone? Explain why.

_____
_____
_____
_____

4. What are your triggers?

_____
_____
_____
_____

5. Do you feel you need to be saved or have you needed to be saved in the past?

_____

_____

_____

_____

_____

6. In which ways? What happened? Explain.

_____

_____

_____

_____

7. What were your results? What better scenario(s) can you create to improve the results?

_____

_____

_____

_____

8. Do you enjoy being alone? Explain.

_____

_____

_____

_____

9. Do you make time for yourself to be alone? How important is it to you? Explain.

_____

_____

_____

_____

10. Do you often feel lonely? Are you fearful of being alone and/or lonely when you are older? Why? Explain.

_____

_____

_____

_____

11. What's an empowering mantra for you to feel safe and secure, comfortable in your own skin? Write a few for different scenarios, for the times of need. Practice them often and feel good.

_____

_____

_____

_____

#25
SELF-CONTROL IS REQUIRED - STAY CALM

Boxing definitely has a part to play in taking away unwanted aggression.
-Joe Calzaghe

The ego says, 'once everything falls into place, I will feel peace,' and the spirit says, 'find your peace and then everything will fall into place.' Act from spirit. People who don't take control of their lives live out of control.
-Jolie Glassman

1. Where and when do you get easily upset? What happens? What are the thoughts you think?

_____

_____

_____

_____

2. What triggers you? Explain.

_____

_____

_____

_____

3. Who triggers you? Explain.

_____

_____

_____

_____

4. How do you feel inside, before you lose control, and after you've lost control?

5. What happens if you lose control when you would rather stay calm?

6. What do you say to yourself when you lose self-control?

7. What are things you can do, or say to yourself, to avoid losing control?

8. What do you need to believe about yourself, and others, to stay calm when it's not conducive to your surroundings or whatever is coming at you?

9. What are some things you can, and will do, to learn better self-control and not get so activated?

#26

NOTHING WORKS WITHOUT INTEGRITY

It's not bragging if you can back it up.
-Muhammad Ali

Whatever areas of your life are not working; integrity is not present. Build and develop your own character. Honor yourself. Honor your words. Be your word. Govern yourself accordingly.
-Jolie Glassman

1. Where is your life working fantastically and you honor yourself?

_____
_____
_____
_____

2. Why do you think this is?

_____
_____
_____

3. Where is your life not working, or not working as well as you would like it to? Why is this the case?

_____
_____
_____

4. Where, and when, are you making promises (in your own head / to yourself) that you are not keeping?

_____
_____
_____

5. What are you doing instead when it becomes time to fulfill these promises?

_____
_____
_____
_____
_____

6. What are dishonoring things you say to yourself that has you not follow through with promises to yourself?

_____
_____
_____
_____

7. Where in life are you not honoring yourself? Your wishes? Your goals?

_____
_____
_____
_____

8. Where in life do you not honor your commitments and promises to others?

_____
_____
_____
_____

9. What happens? What are your results?

_____
_____
_____
_____

10. What are things you must say to yourself to have you follow through and not sell out on yourself and others?

_____
_____
_____
_____

11. Which action steps and ways of being do you need to put into place to have integrity and make things work?

_____
_____
_____
_____

#27

LIFE IS NOT FAIR: PLAY FULL OUT ANYWAY

*Hating people because of their color is wrong. And it doesn't
matter which color does the hating. It's just plain wrong.*
-Muhammad Ali

*Do not let the behavior of others affect your decisions and output of work.
Stay in your lane, and know that even though life is not fair,
you are going to play full out no matter what.*
-Jolie Glassman

1. Where do you feel life is not fair? Explain.

   _____
   _____
   _____
   _____
   _____

2. Are you resigned or cynical in those areas? Explain.

   _____
   _____
   _____
   _____
   _____

3. What are things you say? What are your beliefs in the areas of life not being fair?

   _____
   _____
   _____
   _____
   _____

4. What story could you tell instead, to take action to get unstuck and make a positive difference?

_____

_____

_____

_____

_____

_____

_____

_____

_____

_____

5. Where are you not playing full out? Explain.

_____

_____

_____

_____

_____

_____

_____

_____

_____

_____

6. What holds you back?

_____

_____

_____

_____

_____

_____

_____

_____

_____

_____

7. How can you stop being held back to play full out in these areas and in life?

_____

_____

_____

_____

_____

_____

_____

_____

_____

#28

BE COACHABLE

*I consider myself a student of boxing, a philosopher so to
speak, and my philosophy is to keep learning.*
-Manny Paquiao

*You want to listen and learn as much as possible,
as it is up to you to keep or reject what it is you are hearing and learning.
You decide, but at least be coachable enough to decipher.*
-Jolie Glassman

1. Where do you need coaching? In what areas?
   _____
   _____
   _____
   _____
   _____

2. Where would you like to grow and excel more? Explain.
   _____
   _____
   _____
   _____
   _____

3. What will you do to grow exponentially and succeed in the areas you desire?
   _____
   _____
   _____
   _____
   _____

4. Where in life do you take constructive criticism, and you are coachable?

_____
_____
_____
_____
_____
_____

5. Are there any areas where you are not coachable? Explain.

_____
_____
_____
_____
_____
_____

6. How do you resist when you don't want to accept the coaching?

_____
_____
_____
_____
_____
_____

7. What are things you, or your ego, say to yourself?

_____
_____
_____
_____
_____
_____

8. What are things you can say, and ways of being, so you can imagine the teacher in everything to choose wisely for yourself?

_____
_____
_____
_____
_____

9. Which actions will you take to get coaching in the areas you expressed are needed and most desired?

_____
_____
_____
_____
_____

#29

TOUCH GLOVES,
HONOR, RESPECT

*The thing about boxers is there's respect there. You beat me, and
I may not like it, but you know what, deep down inside,
I respect you. And that's the code of honor.*
-Sugar Ray Leonard

*Without respect and honor for other people, true leadership
becomes ineffective and probably impossible.*
-Jolie Glassman

1. What are some qualities and characteristics you respect and honor in others? Explain.
   _____
   _____
   _____

2. Where do you in your life also possess these qualities and characteristics?
   _____
   _____
   _____

3. Where do you need more honor and respect in your life? What gets in the way?
   _____
   _____
   _____

4. How can you accomplish attaining this?
   _____
   _____
   _____

5. What do you have to stop thinking, saying, and doing to accomplish them?

_____
_____
_____
_____

6. Which areas are working in life where you honor and respect yourself? Explain.

_____
_____
_____
_____

7. What do you do differently in these areas? Explain.

_____
_____
_____
_____

8. What can you apply to the areas you don't honor yourself, that will have you honoring yourself?

_____
_____
_____
_____

9. What are things you do to show you honor yourself?

_____
_____
_____
_____

10. How do you fill up your cup to best give fully to others?

_____
_____
_____

11. What are things you say to yourself when you are not honoring yourself?

_____
_____
_____
_____

12. What are things you say to yourself when you do honor yourself?

_____
_____
_____

#30

HIT AND DON'T GET HIT

You've got to be smart, and not get hit,
and when you're able to do this, you're a fighter.
-Cus D'Amato

The first thing I learned in boxing is to not get hit.
That's the art of boxing. Execute your opponent without getting hit.
-Wladimir Klitchko

In life, you want to be able to attack the task at hand
without getting attacked in return.
-Jolie Glassman

1. Are there areas in life where you leave yourself open to get hurt? Why?

_____

_____

_____

_____

_____

_____

_____

2. What happens?

_____

_____

_____

_____

_____

_____

3. How can you protect yourself better in these situations, and in the future?

_____
_____
_____
_____
_____
_____
_____
_____
_____
_____

4. Which areas are you attacking well, you keep coming forward, and you win?

_____
_____
_____
_____
_____
_____
_____
_____
_____
_____

5. How do you behave in those moments? What has you so formidable in those areas?

_____
_____
_____
_____
_____
_____
_____
_____
_____
_____

6. Practice and rehearse those ways of being. They seem to work.

_____
_____
_____
_____
_____
_____
_____
_____
_____
_____

#31

ALWAYS MOTIVATE YOURSELF

In order to be at the top and maintain your focus you have to have something that motivates you.
-Marvelous Marvin Hagler

Motivation comes after you do what you had said you wanted to do. Motivation is never there when you need it. Make yourself move, as movement is access to motivation. When you feel like quitting, think of why you started.
-Jolie Glassman

1. Which areas of your life are you slacking in?

   _____
   _____
   _____
   _____
   _____

2. What holds you back from being motivated, and producing results in those areas?

   _____
   _____
   _____
   _____

3. What will you begin to do to take action and stop slacking, and how will you make sure to follow through?

   _____
   _____
   _____
   _____

4. Which areas are you motivated and successful?

_____
_____
_____
_____
_____
_____

5. What is it that has you that way?

_____
_____
_____
_____
_____

6. What are things you do to get yourself motivated?

_____
_____
_____
_____
_____

7. What are things you say to yourself that demotivates you and pulls you away from what you said you would do?

_____
_____
_____
_____
_____

8. What can you say instead? What are things you say to yourself that motivates you and propels you into action?

_____
_____
_____
_____
_____

9. What can you take from that and apply to other areas you are slacking in?

_____
_____
_____
_____
_____

#32

HAVE PASSION-LOVE WHAT YOU DO

I've had boxing gloves on since before I could walk, and been in gyms all of my life.
-Floyd Mayweather Jr.

I'm always having fun in training and in boxing.
I think it's because boxing is my passion.
-Manny Pacquiao

My life is fueled by my being, my being fuels the doing, and I come from compassion
and understanding. Without love and passion, what do we have? Passion
unexpressed diminishes. Desire something so badly and then obsess about it.
-Jolie Glassman

1. What are your natural talents and abilities? What tasks or activities do you excel at and enjoy doing even when no one is watching?

    _____
    _____
    _____
    _____

2. What are your values and beliefs? What is important to you, and how can you align what you do with your values?

    _____
    _____
    _____

3. What are your interests and hobbies? How can you incorporate them into your work?

    _____
    _____
    _____

4. What problems or challenges do you enjoy solving? What kind of work would allow you to use your problem-solving skills?

_____

_____

_____

_____

_____

5. What kind of work environment do you thrive in? Do you prefer working independently or collaboratively? In a structured or unstructured environment?

_____

_____

_____

_____

_____

6. What kind of impact do you want to make? How can your work contribute to something meaningful and fulfilling?

_____

_____

_____

_____

_____

7. Is what you're doing now in life your passion and love? Explain why or why not.

_____

_____

_____

_____

8. What needs to change and happen for you to exist with passion, and be at your fullest potential, living your best life? What kind of lifestyle do you want to have and how will you attain it?

_____

_____

_____

_____

9. Which thoughts do you plan to think, and what will you say in order for you to manifest your most passionate life?

_____

_____

_____

_____

#33

MINDSET IS EVERYTHING

When a man says I cannot, he has made a suggestion to himself. He has weakened his power of accomplishing that which otherwise would have been accomplished.
-Muhammad Ali

Anything is possible with the right mindset.
-Tyson Fury

Do things in your mind first and then make your body follow. Create with a mindset that is happy, powerful, abundant, grateful, clear, decisive, positive, and tenacious.
-Jolie Glassman

1. What is your consistent mindset and your disposition? Are you optimistic or pessimistic? Fixed or growth-oriented? Explain.

   _____
   _____
   _____

2. What limiting beliefs do you have about yourself or the world? How can you challenge and overcome these beliefs?

   _____
   _____
   _____

3. What kinds of self-talk do you engage in? Is it positive and encouraging or negative and critical?

   _____
   _____
   _____

4. How do you respond to setbacks and failures? Do you give up easily or persevere through challenges? Explain.

_____
_____
_____
_____

5. How do you view success? Do you see it as something that is achievable with hard work and dedication, or do you believe it is out of reach for you? Explain.

_____
_____
_____
_____

6. In which area of life could you use an upgraded mindset?

_____
_____
_____
_____

7. How/what is your current mindset in this area? What are the thoughts you have about yourself? Others?

_____
_____
_____
_____

8. How would you like your mindset to be? How would you need to think, and what would you say, to get great results?

_____
_____
_____
_____

9. How will you implement this and make it happen? Which actions will you take?

_____
_____
_____
_____

10. What behaviors will you exemplify and when?

_____
_____
_____
_____

#34

DON'T GET BACKED IN THE CORNER, AND WHEN YOU DO, KNOW HOW TO GET OUT

They call it the rope-a-dope. Well, I'm the dope. Ali just laid on the rope and I, like a dope, kept punching until I got tired. But he was probably the most smart fighter I've gotten in the ring with.
-George Foreman

I've got to take the measured steps and avoid the pitfalls. Life in general has pitfalls but being a boxer there's even more.
-Daniel Dubois

There is always a solution. When you find yourself stuck, do not think about how to get out; begin with changing your state, the stuck state. You need to move and change your physiology. Movement is medicine. Then once you get moving and your happy juices and endorphins get flowing, change your story.
-Jolie Glassman

1. Are you feeling stuck in any areas of your life? Which areas, and what is causing it?

    _____

    _____

    _____

    _____

2. Are these common areas for you to be stuck? How long have you been stuck? What are your options and are there any alternative solutions that you haven't considered yet?

    _____

    _____

    _____

    _____

3. How do you think and act when you're feeling stuck?

_____

_____

_____

_____

4. How do you realize you're feeling stuck? Do you say something to yourself or see a specific series of images that keeps you stuck? Explain.

_____

_____

_____

_____

5. How do you get yourself unstuck in these moments? What do you do? What do you say to yourself? What steps do you take to move forward and get out of the corner?

_____

_____

_____

_____

6. What's a challenging area for you where you can still react with ease?

_____

_____

_____

_____

7. How do you think, feel and act in these times?

_____

_____

_____

_____

8. Which phrases and words do you say to yourself?

_____

_____

_____

_____

9. In the area(s) you get stuck, what can you say, feel, act and do instead to get you out of this _stuck_ state? What has worked in the past, and in other areas? Think hard and gather up the insights of your previous successes and ideas to combat this here.

_____

_____

_____

_____

#35
KEEP IT IN THE RING

Sports are sports. It's all about how we carry ourselves out of the ring.
-George Foreman

It would be hard to throw a punch to someone who wasn't a boxer, who wasn't in the ring, and who didn't have on a pair of boxing gloves and who hadn't been training.
-George Foreman

I always say, 'The jails are full because people are treated unfairly.' Play fair and be fair.
-Jolie Glassman

1. Do you feel that you hold grudges? In which ways and towards whom?

_____

_____

_____

_____

_____

2. Do you feel you get over things pretty easily? In which ways and with whom?

_____

_____

_____

_____

_____

_____

3. Do you need to get even with people you feel wronged you? Explain.

_____
_____
_____
_____
_____
_____
_____

4. How do you act, feel, behave and think, when you get confronted, or have a fight/argument?

_____
_____
_____
_____
_____
_____
_____

5. Are those effective, and work for you? Explain.

_____
_____
_____
_____
_____
_____

6. If not, how would you rather act, feel, behave, and think when confronted or have a fight/argument?

_____
_____
_____
_____
_____

7. What can you think, feel, and do in the future when you get triggered?

_____
_____
_____
_____
_____
_____

#36

KNOW WHEN TO PIVOT

To be successful in life you must get in the habit of turning negatives into positives.
-George Foreman

When things are not going in the direction you want,
you need to notice beforehand and pivot.
Do not change the goal; change the direction or actions to get there. Be adaptable.
-Jolie Glassman

1. Is there an area of your life that is not working, and you need to change directions? Which area? Explain what you're doing that's not working.

_____
_____
_____
_____
_____

2. What could you do instead? What different moves can you make to change direction and accomplish all you are after in this area?

_____
_____
_____
_____
_____

3. What have you done in the past when pressured, and needed to change directions?

_____
_____
_____
_____

4. Were you able to pivot in time and get to your finish line? Explain.

_____
_____
_____
_____
_____
_____
_____

5. What is holding you back from changing directions now? Is it the same thing that often holds you back? Explain your thoughts.

_____
_____
_____
_____
_____
_____
_____

6. What are you next steps needed to create change for the better?

_____
_____
_____
_____
_____
_____
_____

7. Who will you need support from, and who will you need to hire or also fire? Metaphorically speaking, not necessarily only in a work environment.

_____
_____
_____
_____
_____
_____

8. When will this happen? In what time frame?

_____
_____
_____
_____
_____

#37

STYLES MAKE FIGHTS

You'd have to say the cleverest fighter in boxing is Mayweather.
He adapts his style against whatever opponent he faces.
-Ricky Hatton

I had an exciting style, I was aggressive, a body puncher, and I attacked all the time.
-Ricky Hatton

In life, have a style that is attractive, engaging, exciting, and able to adjust to
other styles most effectively to come out the winner. Stand out, put your own flare
on things, and be noticeable and unique for the benefit of your own success.
-Jolie Glassman

1. Where do you feel you have the most style and uniqueness?

   _____
   _____
   _____
   _____
   _____
   _____
   _____

2. What is so special about you in this area?

   _____
   _____
   _____
   _____
   _____
   _____

3. What benefits do you get from having this unique flare and style?

_____
_____
_____
_____
_____
_____
_____

4. Where in life do you apply and use this special style and uniqueness?

_____
_____
_____
_____
_____
_____
_____

5. Where else in life could you add some style and flare?

_____
_____
_____
_____
_____
_____
_____

6. What could you add or do differently, to give you a more exciting style, and make your *special sauce* even more special, and achieve greater results in this area? In other areas?

_____
_____
_____
_____
_____

7. What new skills or knowledge would you like to acquire that will facilitate this?

_____
_____
_____
_____
_____

#38

THE PEOPLE IN YOUR CORNER HELP MAKE YOU A CHAMPION, OR NOT

Boxing is individual although there is a team concept, because you need a great corner, you need a great trainer, you need a great prep man, you need all these things.
-Sugar Ray Leonard

When the trainer talks to the fighter, there's a connection.
You don't always have to say much.
-Sugar Ray Leonard

All those around me are the bridge to my success, so they are all important.
-Manny Paquiao

Consistent, helpful, contributive feedback is needed. You do better, and get better results, with people in your corner who are only after your wins.
-Jolie Glassman

1. Who are the people in your corner?

   _____

   _____

   _____

   _____

   _____

2. What about them do you love and admire, that puts them in your corner?

   _____

   _____

   _____

   _____

3. Do you feel you are more successful because of them? In which ways? Why?

_____
_____
_____
_____
_____
_____

4. Can you think of anyone else you would want in your corner?

_____
_____
_____
_____
_____
_____

5. Is it someone you know? If so, who? Is it someone you don't know? If so, who is this person you need to get?

_____
_____
_____
_____
_____
_____

6. What's stopping you from having them in your corner? What do you need to do to have them?

_____
_____
_____
_____
_____
_____

7. What characteristics and abilities do they have, and will they need, to get you to excel much more with them, than without them? Make sure to get your needs met, and then some; it's what makes you a champion, or not.

_____
_____
_____
_____
_____
_____

#39
DON'T BE PREDICTABLE

Assumption is the mother of the screw-ups.
-Angelo Dundee

*When you don't change up a lot,
people may know you a lot better than they should.*
-Evander Holyfield

I always feel like there's no fighter that I can't figure out.
-Roy Jones Jr.

*The moments between the notes create the music.
Never use the same timing, rhythm, or tempo. Do not be predictable.*
-Jolie Glassman

1. Where in life do you make assumptions and end up worrying unnecessarily?

_____

_____

_____

_____

_____

2. What are some of the things you assume?

_____

_____

_____

_____

_____

_____

3. Are they fears? Explain.

_____

_____

_____

_____

_____

4. What ended up happening in these circumstances/situations?

_____

_____

_____

_____

_____

5. How would you like to feel instead when you get overwhelmed in your thinking, and end up worrying unnecessarily?

_____

_____

_____

_____

6. Which thoughts would you want to think and say to yourself instead?

_____

_____

_____

_____

7. Where do you feel your life is mundane and too predictable?

_____

_____

_____

_____

8. What can you do to mix it up?

_____

_____

_____

_____

9. What will you do to mix it up and create some more variety versus predictability for yourself and your life? When? How often?

_____

_____

_____

_____

#40

BE FIRST, BE BRAVE, AND HAVE COURAGE

He who is not courageous enough to take risks will accomplish nothing in life.
–Muhammad Ali

Nothing in life without risk is worthwhile. You must be relentless. That is a winner's quality. If you want to be an anomaly, you need to act like one.
–Jolie Glassman

1. Where in life do you feel brave and courageous?

_____

_____

_____

2. What makes you this way? What do you say to yourself?

_____

_____

_____

3. What is something in your life at this moment that you fear to do, and know you want or need to do it?

_____

_____

_____

4. What exactly holds you back?

_____

_____

_____

5. What are your thoughts, feelings, and beliefs around this?

_____

_____

_____

_____

6. How would you rather be?

_____

_____

_____

_____

7. What thoughts do you need to think, and what new actions would you need to take, to become fearless in the pursuit of what sets your soul on fire, and be able to do what you are fearing to do?

_____

_____

_____

8. What is an experience from your past that is memorable to you, in which you acted courageous, and nothing held you back?

_____

_____

_____

9. Describe how were you being.

_____

_____

_____

10. What thoughts were you thinking?

_____

_____

_____

11. What needs to take place for this situation you're held back in, to move forward now with velocity? How will you move forward and create momentum in these situations where you're being held back?

_____

_____

_____

12. When are you going to do this?

_____

_____

_____

#41

PRAY, HAVE FAITH, AND BELIEVE IN A HIGHER POWER

With God, hard work and focus I can accomplish what is ahead of me.
-Manny Pacquiao

*Prayer is a method practiced from ancient days, so it's very important for
us to maintain a spiritual connection, something that people, gladiators
would do years ago so we're just maintaining that routine.*
-Anthony Joshua

*Pray. Believe. Have faith. Be directed. You are God's child,
and through God all things are possible.
Life and God are always speaking to us. Be silent enough to hear.*
-Jolie Glassman

1. Do you pray, have strong faith, and believe in a higher power?
    _____
    _____
    _____
    _____

2. How do you observe and practice your faith?
    _____
    _____
    _____
    _____

3. Do you meditate? If so, how often and for how long. If not, do you want to? Will you?
    _____
    _____
    _____
    _____

4. Which benefits do you get from meditating? What you are looking to achieve?

_____

_____

_____

_____

5. When do you reserve time for prayer and how often? What do you get out of it? How do you feel?

_____

_____

_____

6. What do you pray for the most and how does it vary?

_____

_____

_____

7. What are your beliefs and faiths?

_____

_____

_____

8. Do they serve you? In which ways?

_____

_____

_____

9. Are there any of your beliefs that don't serve you? What are they?

_____

_____

_____

10. List some of the things you have faith in, and that inspire you.

_____

_____

_____

11. What in life, thus far, do you feel God has taught you?

_____

_____

_____

12. Do you practice silence? What does that look like for you? Do you get value from it? Explain.

_____

_____

_____

#42

BE POSITIVE

I'm one of the most optimistic persons in the world. I always believed that - there's another shot, another chance. In boxing, I never gave up. I kept trying, kept trying. Even when things seemed so dim, I continued to push forward to make something happen in my favor.
-Sugar Ray Leonard

Don't count the days, make the days count.
-Muhammad Ali

Nothing productive comes from negativity except the awareness that positivity is missing and needs to be put in place. It is not the facts that make you miserable, it is your own perception of the facts that make you miserable.
-Jolie Glassman

1. What are you most happy about right now? Excited? Grateful?

    _____
    _____
    _____
    _____

2. What do you enjoy the most now?

    _____
    _____
    _____

3. What do you do that makes you feel good and happy?

    _____
    _____
    _____

4. Do you feel you are a positive person? In which ways?

_____

_____

_____

_____

5. Do you feel others would consider you a positive person? Explain why.

_____

_____

_____

6. What is an area in your life, or situation, where you don't feel so positive?

_____

_____

_____

7. How do you feel instead?

_____

_____

_____

8. What causes you to not feel positive?

_____

_____

_____

9. What are things you say to yourself in the area you don't feel positive?

_____

_____

_____

10. Can you change the story around it? Is it something you can change?

_____

_____

_____

11. What else can you do in this situation to put a positive spin on it? What are thoughts, and actions you can take, to turn this area/situation around and make it into a positive one?

_____

_____

_____

12. How/when will you implement?

_____

_____

_____

#43

HAVE PATIENCE

*Don't worry about the title. Worry about what you got to do today,
tomorrow, the next day and the title will be waiting for you.*
-Anthony Joshua

*Having patience is one of the hardest things about being human. We want to
do it now, and we don't want to wait. Sometimes we miss out on our blessing
when we rush things and do it on our own time.*
-Deontay Wilder

*We need to first be patient with ourselves, and then we can in
turn be patient with others and the world around us.*
-Jolie Glassman

1. Are you a patient person? Do you most often exercise patience when needed? Explain your response.

   _____

   _____

   _____

   _____

2. Where do you easily lose your patience the most? Why do you think that is?

   _____

   _____

   _____

3. Is it a specific scenario? Is it with a specific person? Is it at a specific time of day?

   _____

   _____

   _____

4. Where does this occur, with who, and with what frequency?

_____

_____

_____

5. What happens? How do you react?

_____

_____

_____

6. How does that make you feel after you react in those ways?

_____

_____

_____

7. How would you prefer to act?

_____

_____

_____

8. What needs to happen for you to act this way?

_____

_____

_____

9. Who do you need to be and become, to have patience with yourself?

_____

_____

_____

10. Who do you need to be and become, to have patience with frustrating situations and/ or people?

_____

_____

_____

11. What conversations do you need to have with yourself, and with others?

_____

_____

_____

12. When you *be* this *patient way*, and you practice patience in these situations, or with people, how do you feel?

_____

_____

_____

#44

NEVER TURN YOUR BACK

*I learned to run backwards from Muhammad Ali. He told
me about running backwards because you try to imitate
everything you do in the ring, so sometimes you back-up.*
-Sugar Ray Leonard

*You need to face whatever is in front of you head-on, face-
forward. Go through the storm to get out of it instead of turning
your back because it will blow you over and kill you.*
-Jolie Glassman

1. Is there an area/person in your life that you are turning your back on and avoiding that
    needs to be dealt with, and you just haven't yet? Explain the situation.

    _____
    _____
    _____
    _____
    _____

2. What/Who is it, and what will it take for you to confront it?

    _____
    _____
    _____
    _____

3. What transpired to have you turn your back?

    _____
    _____
    _____
    _____

4. Is it working out the way you want?

_____

_____

_____

_____

5. How would you like it to work out?

_____

_____

_____

_____

6. What needs to happen for it to work out the way you want it to?

_____

_____

_____

7. Can you take responsibility and clean up what is there, so you don't just turn your back? Can you create either a win/win, or an agree to disagree, to have communication and completion in this area or with this person?

_____

_____

_____

8. Do you face your fears head on and accomplish getting through most situations smoothly, or do you turn your back and not deal with it? Explain how it usually plays out.

_____

_____

_____

9. What is the driving force to not turn your back and push through, even though you don't want to?

_____

_____

_____

10. Do you feel others turn their back on you? Explain. In which ways?

_____

_____

_____

11. Do you feel others treat you the way you treat them? Do you see/feel discrepancies? Explain.

_____

_____

_____

#45

TRUST THE PROCESS: SURRENDER

Just take one step at a time, trusting that God still has a plan for you, and He will make the best out of your situation.
-George Foreman

The moments between the notes create the music. Live in your music, surrender, and live life in the now-and then in the now, and then in the now. Life is generated moment by moment, and manifestation happens at the speed of surrender.
-Jolie Glassman

1. Do you feel you are a person that is trusting, and when it is time to surrender you do? Explain.
    _____
    _____
    _____

2. How good are you at surrendering? What does surrendering look like for you, in ways it works for you and your life? Give examples.
    _____
    _____
    _____

3. Where in life do you feel you resist, and are currently resisting?
    _____
    _____
    _____

4. What are your fears around that situation?
    _____
    _____
    _____

5. What would you like to believe to let go and trust the process?

_____

_____

_____

_____

6. Can you practice authentically believing that instead?

_____

_____

_____

_____

7. When was a time in the past, once you let go, *things* began to happen?

_____

_____

_____

8. How did you do it? What did you do?

_____

_____

_____

9. What were things you said to yourself that allowed you to let go?

_____

_____

_____

10. Can you shorten the time it takes to get there to just let go, and trust?

_____

_____

_____

11. What will you need to do to trust and surrender?

_____

_____

_____

12. What will you need to think?

_____

_____

_____

13. How will you need to behave?

_____

_____

_____

#46

DRESS HOW YOU WANT TO BE PERCEIVED

I always designed my robes and how I would present myself at every fight.
-Sugar Ray Leonard

*Create the person you want the world to see. Show the world how you want to be seen.
Present yourself in such a way that is aligned with who you are
and who you want to become.*
-Jolie Glassman

1. Do you dress the way you want to be perceived? Describe your work or most consistent attire.

_____
_____
_____
_____
_____
_____
_____
_____

2. How do you want to be perceived? How do you want people to interpret you from what they see and how you dress?

_____
_____
_____
_____
_____
_____
_____

3. Is the way you dress important to you? Why or why not?

4. Are you fully self-expressed in the way you present yourself? Why or why not?

5. What is missing, or what can be added, to align yourself in the way you dress, with your brand, and who you want to be perceived as in the world?

6. Who are your fashion role models? Who do you want to be like in dress, style and presentation? Why? What is so appealing to you?

#47

FEEL — YOU NEED TO MOURN

You need to mourn, you need to be upset, to give yourself time to replenish.
Then you use it all as fuel to get stronger.
-Anthony Yarde

We live in a world of contrast and polarity, and then we seek balance.
Feel your emotions so they can pass. If you do not want something to persist,
then do not resist its existence and presence.
-Jolie Glassman

1. Do you mourn things in your life that are sad or do you just brush it under the rug? How do you mourn?

   _____
   _____
   _____
   _____

2. Do you have pent up anger or frustration or do you let things out along the way? Explain.

   _____
   _____
   _____
   _____

3. Which area or with whom, are you holding back anger and frustration from not dealing with it?

   _____
   _____
   _____
   _____

4. How do you plan to deal with your anger and frustration?

_____

_____

_____

_____

_____

_____

5. What do you still need to mourn, which you have not?

_____

_____

_____

_____

_____

_____

6. What has held you back from mourning?

_____

_____

_____

_____

_____

_____

7. How does it make you feel? Express yourself fully.

_____

_____

_____

_____

_____

8. What do you want to happen? How would you rather feel?

_____

_____

_____

_____

_____

9. Which actions will you take to have what you want, and feel what you want to feel?

_____

_____

_____

_____

_____

#48

TIMING IS EVERYTHING

Not only do I knock them out...but I pick the round.
-Muhammad Ali

Do not wait for the right time; create and find the right time and capitalize on it. Time things to win. People and their actions have patterns. Notice them beforehand and time things accordingly to best accomplish what you are setting out to achieve.
-Jolie Glassman

1. Do you time things well in life? Give examples.

_____

_____

_____

2. Name a time things could have been really great, but the timing was just not good?

_____

_____

_____

3. What happened that was so great?

_____

_____

_____

_____

_____

4. What about it determined the timing was not right?

_____
_____
_____
_____
_____

5. When was a time you felt the timing was just perfect and you needed to take action?

_____
_____
_____
_____
_____

6. What happened that was so great?

_____
_____
_____
_____
_____

7. What about it determined it was the right time?

_____
_____
_____
_____

8. What was the difference in your feelings when it was not the right time, compared to when it was the perfect time?

_____
_____
_____
_____

9. Are you clear when the timing is right or not for situations you want to engage? Explain.

_____
_____
_____
_____

10. If you are not fully clear, where is the confusion?

_____
_____
_____
_____

#49
MUST BE PRESENT AT ALL TIMES

All the time he's boxing, he's thinking.
All the time he was thinking, I was hitting him.
-Jack Dempsey

Get out of the habit of thinking of what you are going to say and do next, as you can do that when you get there. Become one with what you are doing. The present moment is where all wisdom is revealed and where performance is at its best.
-Jolie Glassman

1. What does *being present* mean to you? What does that look like for you?

   _____
   _____
   _____
   _____

2. Are you very present at most times? Explain your answer.

   _____
   _____
   _____
   _____

3. Do you often do things and realize you are not present? How often?

   _____
   _____
   _____

4. What activities and tasks do you do mindlessly, *without* presence?

   _____
   _____
   _____

5. Which activities and tasks do you complete *with* presence, and you cannot be mindless or sidetracked?

_____

_____

_____

_____

6. What is the difference for you, your thoughts, and your feelings regarding what you can do mindlessly, versus things you have to be fully present?

_____

_____

_____

_____

7. Which activity or task can you perform with more presence, that will make all the difference in the results you produce?

_____

_____

_____

_____

8. Where do you want to be more present in life where you are not? List the areas and situations.

_____

_____

_____

_____

9. What do you need to put in, and what do you need to take out, to accomplish more presence where you're currently not?

_____

_____

_____

_____

10. Do you have a meditation routine? If not, are you willing to begin one daily?

_____

_____

_____

11. Practice presence. Begin with setting a timer for five minutes, sit up straight, breath fully and deeply, and stare into a flame of a lit candle. Let your mind command your body to stay.

_____

_____

_____

#50

ALWAYS BE READY

*The same hand that can write a beautiful poem,
can knock you out with one punch - that's poetic justice.*
-"Irish" Wayne Kelly

*Fitness is a state of readiness. When you are fit, you are ready. The
more you are prepared, the more value you get out of what is coming
your way. When you anticipate crisis, change will be a gift.*
-Jolie Glassman

1. Do you consider yourself a *fit* person? *Fit* meaning you are ready for whatever comes
    your way. Do you consider yourself strong in life and always ready? State reasons for
    your answer.

    _____
    _____
    _____
    _____

2. Describe a few scenarios where you were well prepared, strong, and fit for what was
    coming your way, and made it through like a champ?

    _____
    _____
    _____
    _____

3. Think and recall some of the phrases you said to yourself that pushed you through to
    be fit, strong, and ready. State them here.

    _____
    _____
    _____

4. How did you move about? What did your body do in those moments you were ready, well prepared, strong, and fit?

_____

_____

_____

5. Describe something you are going through where you do *not* feel fit, strong, and ready.

_____

_____

_____

6. What is missing for you to be ready in this area and in other areas in your life?

_____

_____

_____

7. How are you moving your body about in this situation? What things are you saying to yourself?

_____

_____

_____

8. How can you move your body instead? What are things you can say to yourself that will move you in the direction of being in a state of readiness *now*, for this situation?

_____

_____

_____

9. What can you do and add into your life, to increase your state of readiness, *to always be ready*?

_____

_____

_____

10. What are some of the things you do currently that hold you back from being in a constant state of readiness?

_____

_____

_____

11. What are phrases you will say to yourself to be/exist in a state of readiness? How will you move your body? *How will you always be ready and be F.I.T. and Fight for Intentional Transformation, From, Love?*

_____

_____

_____

#51
PREPARE FOR THE UNEXPECTED

I always expect challenges. Boxing is not an easy sport.
-Sugar Ray Leonard

Anticipation is power. Leaders anticipate; losers react. Know the road ahead.
-Jolie Glassman

1. Do you feel prepared for whatever comes your way? How? In what ways?

   _____
   _____
   _____
   _____
   _____
   _____

2. When was a time you were blind-sided, and had a setback, in which you felt it could have been avoided had you done, or known something different? Explain.

   _____
   _____
   _____
   _____
   _____
   _____

3. What could you have done, or known, instead to prevent that setback?

   _____
   _____
   _____
   _____
   _____

4. What did you learn from it?

_____
_____
_____
_____
_____
_____
_____
_____
_____

5. Is there anything you do differently because of it? What?

_____
_____
_____
_____
_____
_____
_____

6. When was a time in your life you were prepared for the unexpected, and got through it all like a champ? What did you do that prepared you so well? What were your ways of being and how were you feeling? What were things you would say to yourself?

_____
_____
_____
_____
_____
_____
_____
_____

7. What are things you can do, and ways you can strengthen, to prepare for the unexpected? Write down at least 4 things/ways. Remember, success leaves clues.

_____
_____
_____
_____
_____
_____
_____
_____

#52

PLAY BIG

I want to be the best. Not just the best fighter. I want to be the best athlete,
period. When I leave, I will be known as TBE and that's The Best Ever.
-Floyd Mayweather Jr.

You cannot succeed at things if you do not fail along the way. Failing is
part of the journey, and it is not a destination unless you give up.
-Jolie Glassman

1. What does *play big* mean to you, and what does it look like for you and in your life?

   _____
   _____
   _____
   _____

2. Do you *play big* in your life endeavors? Explain.

   _____
   _____
   _____
   _____

3. Could you play bigger? Explain how. In which areas and ways?

   _____
   _____
   _____

4. What prevents you from playing big?

   _____
   _____
   _____

5. Explain a time that you played *big* and it paid off immensely?

_____

_____

_____

6. Explain a time you did not play big, and you regret that you didn't, and you lost out?

_____

_____

_____

7. What is missing for you to play big in the areas you would like to, and you don't?

_____

_____

_____

8. What exactly do you say to yourself? How do you move your body about in these areas?

_____

_____

_____

9. What would you prefer to say to yourself in these areas that would inspire you to take massive action?

_____

_____

_____

10. What actions will you take to play big in at least one area?

_____

_____

_____

11. What will you no longer say to yourself?

_____

_____

_____

12. What will you no longer do?

_____

_____

_____

13. In the area you will play big, how will a day in your life look in this area? How will it look in six months? In one year? In five years?

_____

_____

_____

#53

APPRECIATE — HAVE GRATITUDE

*Everything I have in this world, I owe to the sport
of boxing, and I won't ever forget that.*
-Oscar De La Hoya

*I consider myself blessed. I consider you blessed. We've
all been blessed with God-given talents.*
-Sugar Ray Leonard

*Appreciate the little things, and then the little things will become
big things. Recognize the full worth of something, as the palace
of happiness rests on the grounds of gratitude.*
-Jolie Glassman

1. Do you consider yourself to be a grateful person? Explain. How do you practice gratitude daily?

   _____

   _____

   _____

2. Are you able to cultivate the feeling of *gratitude* at any time? What are your specific practices to be grateful when you are not feeling so great?

   _____

   _____

   _____

3. List 20 things you are grateful for, and why and how each make you feel grateful.

   _____

   _____

   _____

4. List 20 people you are grateful for, and why and how each make you feel grateful.

_____
_____
_____
_____
_____
_____

5. Which area do you not feel grateful?

_____
_____
_____
_____

6. How do you feel about this area?

_____
_____
_____
_____

7. What would it take for you to shift it into a feeling of appreciation and gratitude?

_____
_____
_____
_____
_____

8. What would you have to believe?

_____
_____
_____
_____
_____

9. Can you practice what will transform it? Will you? How often?

_____
_____
_____
_____
_____

10. Bring those feelings from the things and people you are grateful for into this area. Practice feeling gratitude and appreciation. Find ways to be grateful in any/all situations. List 5 new things you can do daily to cultivate more gratitude in your life. Will you do them?

_____
_____
_____
_____

#54

DON'T WORRY ABOUT
WHAT OTHERS ARE DOING

*I don't need to worry about what other people are talking
about me. Instead, I focus on the people talking positive
and all the positive things that I know I am doing.*
-Anthony Yarde

*Comparison is the thief of all joy. When you spend your time
focusing on other people, you give them energy over you. You
give them power. Where focus goes, energy flows. Learn to
focus on yourself and not on what others are doing.*
-Jolie Glassman

1. How much time, down to the minute, do you spend scrolling through social media daily?

_____
_____
_____
_____
_____
_____

2. How do you feel while doing that, and how do you feel after?

_____
_____
_____
_____
_____
_____

3. Who in life do you focus on that doesn't help you grow or add value to your life? List at least five examples.

_____

_____

_____

_____

_____

_____

_____

_____

4. What about them has you give them attention?

_____

_____

_____

_____

_____

_____

_____

5. What does this mean for you? What are your thoughts, and feelings about yourself?

_____

_____

_____

_____

_____

_____

6. What can you do to not have this distraction and make it positive instead? List at least 5 things.

_____

_____

_____

_____

_____

_____

7. How will you monitor and hold yourself accountable to not worry and focus on these futile people or situations?

_____

_____

_____

_____

_____

_____

#55

BE VIGILANT, KEEP YOUR HANDS UP, AND PROTECT YOURSELF AT ALL TIMES

Everyone has a plan 'til they get punched in the face.
-Mike Tyson

Learn how to defend yourself in many ways against many things – not to be in fear of them but to be empowered in your defenses against them. Knowledge is potential power; gather it up and use it accordingly.
-Jolie Glassman

1. Do you know how to protect yourself? Physically? Financially? Emotionally? Mentally? Spiritually? In life? Explain your response for each area.

_____
_____
_____
_____
_____
_____
_____

2. What is something you want to learn to be better protected? Physically? Financially? Emotionally? Mentally? Spiritually? In life? Explain your response for each area.

_____
_____
_____
_____
_____
_____
_____

3. Name a time you got blind-sided, and wish you could have protected yourself better to get different results. What happened?

4. What could you have done for that not to have happened?

5. When was a time you were vigilant, and you protected yourself in a way that you were safe and triumphant? Physically? Financially? Emotionally? Mentally? Spiritually? In life? Explain your response for each area.

6. What are your strengths and weaknesses that have you vigilant and ultra-aware?

7. What will you learn, or do differently and consistently, to have you more vigilant and protected in one or more of those areas?

#56

BALANCE IS EVERYTHING

Focus on being balanced - success is balance.
-Laila Ali

Have routines that serve you, stabilize you, and help you create balance in your life. Know your needs and give them to yourself.
-Jolie Glassman

1. Where in life are you out of balance?
   _____
   _____
   _____
   _____
   _____
   _____

2. Has it ever been balanced in this area before? When?
   _____
   _____
   _____
   _____
   _____
   _____

3. Which areas in your life are balanced?
   _____
   _____
   _____
   _____
   _____

4. What is missing, in regards to who you're being, or what you're doing, that has you out of balance in the specific area(s)?

_____
_____
_____
_____
_____

5. What are your emotions around these areas of imbalance and balance? Describe how you feel, move about, and speak differently in these areas.

_____
_____
_____
_____
_____

6. Do you feel/believe balance is possible in the areas you lack it? Explain your reasoning.

_____
_____
_____
_____
_____

7. What do you want to happen, where you are not fulfilling, and/or making excuses why you can't have it… *all*, to have balance? Describe how these areas of imbalance would be different if you were balanced.

_____
_____
_____
_____
_____

8. What needs to happen, and who do you need to be/become, to have balance in all areas?

_____
_____
_____
_____

9. What boundaries do you need to create for yourself, and with others? List at least 3 for each.

_____
_____
_____
_____

#57

REMEMBER WHERE YOU CAME FROM, AND IT DOESN'T HAVE TO BE WHERE YOU'RE GOING

I remember as a little boy I ate one meal a day and sometimes slept in the street. I will never forget that, and it inspires me to fight hard, stay strong, and remember all the people of my country, trying to achieve better for themselves.
-Manny Paquiao

When people see what I have now, they have no idea where I came from and how I didn't have anything growing up.
-Floyd Mayweather Jr.

If my mom was the mother I hoped she would be, I would not be the woman I am. God gave me exactly what I needed to be me; and therefore, I thank my mom every day, and I choose my mom for all the good, bad, and ugly.
-Jolie Glassman

1. What is your story? Where do you come from?

_____

_____

_____

_____

_____

2. Does it empower you or disempower you? Explain.

_____

_____

_____

_____

3. What are parts that disempower you?

_____

_____

_____

_____

4. How can you reframe those parts to empower you? Write them here.

_____

_____

_____

_____

5. Which struggles from your past made you into the great person you are?

_____

_____

_____

_____

6. What have you learned from them?

_____

_____

_____

_____

7. What about them made you great?

_____

_____

_____

_____

8. Who from your past are you grateful for and will always remember? List at least 5 people.

_____

_____

_____

_____

9. Where are you going? What is your plan for where you're heading? In the next 6 months? In one year? In five years? Ultimately when you are older?

_____

_____

_____

10. How does your past help to get where you are heading? In what ways?

_____

_____

_____

#58

FIND AND CREATE OPENINGS

Within our dreams and aspirations, we find our opportunities.
-Sugar Ray Leonard

If you keep knocking you will find open doors, and if there is no door, make a door. You do not have to close one door for another one to open. There are never-ending possibilities and openings; you just need to seek and find them.
-Jolie Glassman

1. Where in life do you feel stuck?

_____
_____
_____
_____
_____
_____

2. What are you currently doing, and not doing, that has you stuck?

_____
_____
_____
_____
_____

3. What are some things you can do in that area to create movement?

_____
_____
_____
_____
_____

4. What is holding you back?

_____
_____
_____
_____
_____
_____
_____

5. What is one thing, and the very next thing, you can do to move the needle forward?

_____
_____
_____
_____
_____
_____
_____

6. When was a time in the past you felt stuck?

_____
_____
_____
_____
_____
_____
_____

7. What did you to resolve it and get unstuck?

_____
_____
_____
_____
_____

8. Can you apply the same mindset to get unstuck here, or what can you create? What is the mindset you need to create to get unstuck, and what are some things you can say to inspire yourself?

_____
_____
_____
_____
_____

#59

MAKE YOURSELF COMFORTABLE
WITH THE UNCOMFORTABLE

Boxing is the ultimate challenge. There's nothing that can compare to testing yourself the way you do every time you step in the ring.
-Sugar Ray Leonard

Comfort is a place of power compared to discomfort, which is not a place of power. Always stand in power, comfortably, no matter what. Practice 'til you can make what's uncomfortable, comfortable.
-Jolie Glassman

1. What are things you do each day that are uncomfortable and you don't love doing?

_____
_____
_____
_____
_____

2. What is the reason/incentive that motivates you to get them done?

_____
_____
_____
_____

3. What are things you know you need to do but you avoid them?

_____
_____
_____
_____

4. What are you resisting currently, and what would it look like to not resist?

_____
_____
_____
_____
_____
_____

5. What gets in the way?

_____
_____
_____
_____
_____

6. What is something you want badly but you don't go after it as you have excuses why not to? What are your excuses that have you not get it done?

_____
_____
_____
_____
_____

7. What actions can you take today to start getting it done?

_____
_____
_____
_____
_____

8. What do you need to move out of the way to accomplish this? What things do you need to say to yourself, and how will you need to move your body, to get it done?

_____
_____
_____
_____
_____

9. Will you do it? What will you put into place to get it done? By when?

_____
_____
_____
_____
_____

#60

FIGHT YOUR HEART OUT —
BOXERS ARE ALL HEART

A champion is someone who gets up when he can't.
-Jack Dempsey

Who you are is in your heart. Where you live is in your head. Cultivate both. Lead and come from your heart yet take your brain with you. The brain thinks, and the heart knows. Our hearts are the bridge to oneness, the seat of the soul.
-Jolie Glassman

1. When it's time to fight for what's important to you, do you? Explain why you feel this way and how you go about it.

_____
_____
_____
_____
_____

2. Do you often give up or push through? What happens?

_____
_____
_____
_____

3. Which area do you feel could use a little more fight?

_____
_____
_____
_____

4. Where are you selling yourself short and you know you can be/do/have so much more?

_____
_____
_____
_____
_____

5. What are things you can do, and actions you can take, to push harder?

_____
_____
_____
_____
_____

6. When was a time you gave it your all, even more than you imagined you could?

_____
_____
_____
_____
_____

7. What did you do? How did you feel? What were things you said to yourself, that had you not give up and push so hard?

_____
_____
_____
_____

8. Where else can you apply those ways of being?

_____
_____
_____
_____

9. Which actions will you take and in what areas?

_____
_____
_____
_____

10. When will you begin and with what frequency?

_____
_____
_____
_____

#61

BE AN AMAZING PROBLEM SOLVER

There's one thing I don't ever think about: losing. Instead, I think about how I'm going to win, and how I can do it the quickest way.
-Joe Frazier

Be obsessed with expanding, growing, and serving. The bigger the problem is, the greater the reward will be when you solve it. Keep your eye on the desired outcome and do the right things along the way to get there. The size of the hero is determined by the size of the opponent. Have big problems worth fighting for and be the problem-solving hero of your own life. To solve a problem, you need to remove the cause, not the symptom.
-Jolie Glassman

1. Describe a situation where you had to solve a problem.

_____

_____

_____

2. What did you do?

_____

_____

_____

3. What was the result?

_____

_____

_____

4. What might you have done differently?

_____

_____

5. Give an example of a situation in which you saw an opportunity in a potential problem.

_____

_____

_____

6. What did you do?

_____

_____

_____

7. What was the outcome?

_____

_____

_____

8. What steps do you take before making a decision on how to solve a problem? Why?

_____

_____

_____

9. Describe a time where you developed a different problem-solving approach.

_____

_____

_____

10. What steps did you follow?

_____

_____

_____

11. Write about a time when you became aware of a potential problem and resolved it before it became an issue.

_____

_____

_____

12. What are some of the problems you are currently facing?

_____

_____

13. What skills and knowledge do you need to acquire in order to solve them?

_____

_____

14. What opportunities could you obtain from solving these problems?

_____

_____

#62

SHOW NO PAIN

A sight game is that I am hurt, but I aim to make you believe that I am not even hurt, and with this confidence appearing on my face, I don't panic otherwise your opponent will know that you are hurt. That's the whole art game in boxing.
-Evander Holyfield

Focus on the prize, not the pain. Pain is part of life, so just process it, move forward and get on with it.
-Jolie Glassman

1. When was a time you felt a lot of pain? Physically? Emotionally?

    _____
    _____
    _____
    _____
    _____

2. What did you do to get through it?

    _____
    _____
    _____
    _____
    _____

3. What did you learn and how could you have gotten through it more seamlessly?

    _____
    _____
    _____
    _____
    _____

4. What is something painful that you are dealing with now?

_____
_____
_____
_____
_____
_____
_____

5. How are you processing it and what are you doing to get through it? What are things you are saying to yourself? What can you say to yourself to best process and go through it smoothly?

_____
_____
_____
_____
_____
_____
_____
_____

6. What are some tactics you use to get through a painful situation?

_____
_____
_____
_____
_____
_____
_____
_____

7. What can you do in the future to process pain in a way that's not so obvious?

_____
_____
_____
_____
_____
_____

8. Who would you need to be in order to show no pain, and how would you go about it?

_____
_____
_____
_____
_____
_____

#63

FIGHT TO YOUR STRENGTHS: USE YOUR ASSETS, YOUR BEST TOOLS

Everybody is blessed with a certain talent; you have to know what that talent is. You have to maximize it and push it to the limit.
-Floyd Mayweather Jr.

I've always said that the best version of me can beat anyone in the world, and as long as the best version of me steps through those ropes, I can use my strengths to take away his strengths.
-Callum Smith

Fine tune your strengths because they are your assets. Know what you are good at and get greater.
-Jolie Glassman

1. What are your best talents, tools, and strengths?

   _____
   _____
   _____
   _____
   _____

2. What do you do in your career/job/worklife that exemplifies your strengths?

   _____
   _____
   _____
   _____
   _____

3. Is there anything else you could be doing or creating that would showcase your strengths?

    _____
    _____
    _____
    _____
    _____
    _____
    _____
    _____

4. What are some of your strengths that need to be even stronger?

    _____
    _____
    _____
    _____
    _____
    _____

5. Which courses, books, tools and actions can you take to get better in these areas?

    _____
    _____
    _____
    _____
    _____
    _____
    _____

6. Do you use your best assets and strengths? Are they showcased?

    _____
    _____
    _____
    _____
    _____

7. Who do you need to become to use your best strengths, tools, and assets? What do you need to believe about yourself to be the strongest in your best areas?

    _____
    _____
    _____
    _____
    _____
    _____

#64

ALWAYS HAVE A PLAN, AND BACK-UP PLANS AS WELL

I play chess for about four hours a day in training camp.
You have to decide what move to use, or what combination of moves.
-Lennox Lewis

Good ideas do not find you. Prepare, make plans, and go after all you need to
accomplish. Prepare yourself to be ready for challenge, fortune, and opportunity.
Be well equipped to be really valuable.
-Jolie Glassman

1. Which area in your life would be so much better and efficient if you brought systems and organization into it?

    _____
    _____
    _____
    _____
    _____

2. What are you currently doing in the area of planning that *is* working?

    _____
    _____
    _____
    _____

3. What is not working? What has you out of your flow that could use better planning and pre-thinking?

    _____
    _____
    _____
    _____

4. What are things you can learn and do to become sharper and clearer?

_____
_____
_____
_____
_____
_____
_____

5. How could you reach more people this year in comparison to last year?

_____
_____
_____
_____
_____
_____
_____

6. _Remember to use SMART goals for all this planning: Specific, Measurable, Achievable, Realistic, and anchored within a TIME frame._ List at least three SMART goals here for yourself that you will accomplish in the next six months.

_____
_____
_____
_____
_____
_____

7. Who do you need to be? How will you feel and behave? Which actions will you take with presence while behaving in these new ways?

_____
_____
_____
_____
_____
_____

8. How does your life look? How do you feel when you have plans and back-up plans?

_____
_____
_____
_____
_____

#65

DON'T LOSE FOCUS: KEEP YOUR EYES ON THE TARGET

Keep your focus on what matters the most.
-Manny Paquiao

Look forward with eyes wide opened, and do not take them off the target. In your mind, you can transform anything with your words, integrity, and focus. Wherever focus goes, energy flows. Focus on the outcome and the results you want to achieve.
-Jolie Glassman

1. Do you feel you have a strong focus? Do you keep your eyes on the target? Explain why you answered the way you did.

   _____
   _____
   _____
   _____
   _____

2. Which area in your life could use more focus and attention?

   _____
   _____
   _____
   _____
   _____

3. What has been in the way of your focus?

   _____
   _____
   _____
   _____

4. How do you feel when you want to focus, yet do not? What distractions do you create and which behaviors do you exemplify that make you unfocused?

_____

_____

_____

_____

_____

_____

5. How would you rather feel? What are things you can/will do instead?

_____

_____

_____

_____

_____

_____

6. Why are you interested in this area to begin with? What is the goal?

_____

_____

_____

_____

_____

_____

7. Visualize how you want to be. What will this situation look like if you do not take your eyes off the target, and you focus fully? What does focus and eyes on the target look like for you?

_____

_____

_____

_____

_____

8. Who do you need to be, and what practices will you put in place, to _be your future self now_ and live that visualization _now,_ and be super focused? What phrases will you say to yourself to focus and follow through fully?

_____

_____

_____

_____

_____

_____

#66

REFUSE TO LOSE

I refuse to be beat.
-Mike Tyson

Remove losing as an option. You win or learn.
Disappointment either drives us or destroys us. Let it drive you.
-Jolie Glassman

1. When was a time you *won*?

_____

_____

_____

_____

_____

_____

2. What was it about and what did you get out of it?

_____

_____

_____

_____

_____

_____

3. What motivated you to compete and win?

_____

_____

_____

_____

_____

4. Who did you need to be to accomplish the win? What were things you said to yourself to push yourself and win?

_____
_____
_____
_____
_____
_____

5. How did you feel during the process and once you *won*?

_____
_____
_____
_____
_____

6. Do you feel like you are *losing* in any area of life? Explain where.

_____
_____
_____
_____
_____

7. Which habits, behaviors, and emotions can you apply that were present when you won?

_____
_____
_____
_____
_____

8. Who do you need to become to refuse to lose and always win or learn?

_____
_____
_____
_____
_____

9. What mantras or tools will you use when you are losing to switch it up and create/find the win?

_____
_____
_____
_____
_____

#67

LEARN WHO YOUR REAL FRIENDS ARE

Everybody you fight is not your enemy,
and everybody that helps you is not your friend.
-Mike Tyson

Notice who is in your locker room after you lose, not after you win.
-Angelo Dundee

Learn to be your own best friend, and you will only accept others who align.
-Jolie Glassman

1. Who do you consider your *real* friends?
    _____
    _____
    _____
    _____
    _____

2. How long have they been your *real* friends?
    _____
    _____
    _____
    _____
    _____

3. Which qualities do they possess to constitute being a real friend?
    _____
    _____
    _____
    _____

4. Which qualities do you possess that make you a *real* friend?

_____

_____

_____

_____

_____

_____

_____

_____

_____

5. Which qualities are deal breakers to being your close friend?

_____

_____

_____

_____

_____

_____

_____

_____

_____

6. Which qualities are most important to you in a *real* friend?

_____

_____

_____

_____

_____

_____

_____

_____

_____

7. Which ways of being and qualities can you possess, to be an even better friend?

_____

_____

_____

_____

_____

_____

_____

_____

_____

#68

BE SUPER DISCIPLINED AND DEDICATED

Discipline is doing what you hate to do but doing it like you love it.
-Mike Tyson

*We need to do all we need to do, whatever it takes, to get to where we want to be,
and act accordingly. We must work the muscle of not wanting to do it
and then doing it anyway, with as little lag time as possible.*
-Jolie Glassman

1. What does it *feel* like when you are super dedicated and disciplined? Conjure your fantasies and *feel the feelings now*.

   _____
   _____
   _____
   _____

2. Where in life are you lacking dedication and discipline?

   _____
   _____
   _____
   _____

3. What are your fears around that situation?

   _____
   _____
   _____

4. What would you like to believe instead?

   _____
   _____
   _____

5. Can you practice believing that authentically? Explain.

_____

_____

_____

6. When was a time in the past where you were super disciplined and dedicated?

_____

_____

_____

7. How did you do it then?

_____

_____

_____

8. What exactly did you do?

_____

_____

_____

9. What were things you said to yourself that had you dedicated and disciplined?

_____

_____

_____

10. Can you shorten the time it takes to get there, and just get super disciplined and dedicated?

_____

_____

_____

11. What will you need to do?

_____

_____

_____

12. What will you need to think?

_____

_____

_____

_____

13. How will you need to behave?

_____

_____

_____

#69

WHEN PEOPLE TELL YOU THAT YOU CAN'T DO IT, PROVE THEM WRONG

Thank you to every person who has told me I can't.
You are just another reason I will.
-Manny Paquiao

When someone says you can't do something, say, 'Yet.' It may not be
easy, and almost never is, yet for sure it is possible. Find someone who has
accomplished what you want, in the ways that you want, and follow them.
-Jolie Glassman

1. Describe a time when you excelled at something, and people didn't believe you would or could.

   _____
   _____
   _____
   _____

2. What was the outcome? What did you do to prove them wrong?

   _____
   _____
   _____
   _____

3. Who did you need to be in order to accomplish this?

   _____
   _____
   _____
   _____

4. Where in life do you need to excel and strive more?

_____
_____
_____
_____
_____
_____

5. What is holding you back?

_____
_____
_____
_____
_____
_____

6. Do you believe you can accomplish it? Explain your response.

_____
_____
_____
_____
_____
_____

7. Which people do you need around you? Who do you need support from or to hire?

_____
_____
_____
_____
_____

8. How do you need to *be?* What do you need to do?

_____
_____
_____
_____
_____

9. When will you do these things by, and with what frequency?

_____
_____
_____
_____
_____

#70

NEVER GIVE UP

You never lose, till you actually give up.
-Mike Tyson

*Say to yourself, 'No matter what happens, I got this, and I
am not giving up.' Make giving up not an option.*
-Jolie Glassman

1. Do you push past your limits and never give up? Explain.

_____
_____
_____
_____
_____
_____

2. Which area of your life do you feel like you want to give up?

_____
_____
_____
_____
_____
_____

3. What is so difficult?

_____
_____
_____
_____
_____

4. What is missing or what can you add to change the situation or story?

_____

_____

_____

_____

_____

_____

_____

5. When was a time you pushed really hard, never gave up, and came out the winner?

_____

_____

_____

_____

_____

_____

_____

6. How did you feel? What did it take for you to win?

_____

_____

_____

_____

_____

_____

_____

7. Can you apply those feelings and intentions to other areas where you're not pushing yourself as hard and as far as you'd like? Explain how you will do it.

_____

_____

_____

_____

_____

8. What new feelings, mantras, and actions will you take to excel in the area(s) you do not shine in? Be specific and make deadlines.

_____

_____

_____

_____

_____

#71

BE IN FLOW

Float like a butterfly, sting like a bee.
The hands can't hit what the eyes can't see.
-Muhammad Ali

My philosophy of life and fitness is it's the moments between the notes that create
the music. Life is a collection of moments; be in the flow of them. It is always about
getting to the space in between and playing in the space between the two polarities.
-Jolie Glassman

1. What is an area of your life that is weighing you down? Explain why.
    _____
    _____
    _____
    _____

2. Are you sure everything you believe here is the truth? How do you know?
    _____
    _____
    _____
    _____

3. Could there be another scenario?
    _____
    _____
    _____

4. What else could this mean?
    _____
    _____
    _____

5. Is this problem still going to exist next week? Next month? Next year?

_____

_____

_____

_____

6. Is it solvable? Explain.

_____

_____

_____

_____

7. What does it look like, and how do you feel, when you are in flow?

_____

_____

_____

_____

8. What are things you say to yourself and what are your beliefs when you are in flow?

_____

_____

_____

_____

9. Which characteristics can you apply and use to create flow in the area weighing you down?

_____

_____

_____

_____

10. On a scale of one to ten, how well do you flow through life and avoid getting caught up in circumstances that seem to be unsolvable? Explain your response with ten being the greatest.

_____

_____

_____

_____

11. List some things you can do, habits you can create, and ways of being you can rehearse and adopt, to get that number higher and flow more through life without getting stuck unnecessarily.

_____

_____

_____

_____

#72

LEAVE IT ALL IN THE RING — GIVE IT YOUR ALL

*If I lose, I'll walk away and never feel bad because I did all I could.
There was nothing more to do.*
-Joe Frazier

*You will never feel the disappointment of 'I should have tried
harder' if you did the best you could from the start. All you can
do is do your best, so make sure you do that, always.*
-Jolie Glassman

1. When was a time you gave it your all and got great results?

_____
_____
_____
_____
_____

2. What did you do, and how did you push yourself to give it your all?

_____
_____
_____
_____
_____

3. Which things would you say to yourself to push through and give it your all?

_____
_____
_____
_____
_____

4. Which area of life needs more attention and effort from you?

_____

_____

_____

_____

_____

_____

5. How do you want that area to be and how would it be if you gave it your all?

_____

_____

_____

_____

_____

_____

6. What is missing? What can you do differently to be more inclined to give it your all?

_____

_____

_____

_____

_____

7. Who do you need to be, and what new habits do you need to implement?

_____

_____

_____

_____

_____

8. What are things you can say to yourself that will motivate you to keep pushing through and give it your all?

_____

_____

_____

_____

_____

9. When will you start and what actions will you take?

_____

_____

_____

_____

_____

#73

YOU WILL BECOME HUMBLE

If you're not humble, it's going to bring humbleness to you.
-Mike Tyson

You cannot live as if you are better than anyone else because the only person you want to be better than is the person you were yesterday.
-Jolie Glassman

1. How do you define *being humble*?

_____
_____
_____
_____
_____
_____

2. Do you consider yourself humble?

_____
_____
_____
_____
_____
_____

3. What makes you humble or not?

_____
_____
_____
_____
_____

4. Who do you admire in life that exudes humility to you?

_____
_____
_____
_____
_____
_____
_____
_____

5. What are some areas you exemplify humility?

_____
_____
_____
_____
_____
_____
_____

6. Where else in life could you be even more humble?

_____
_____
_____
_____
_____
_____
_____

7. How do you train yourself to be humble?

_____
_____
_____
_____
_____
_____
_____

8. Why is it important to be humble?

_____
_____
_____
_____
_____

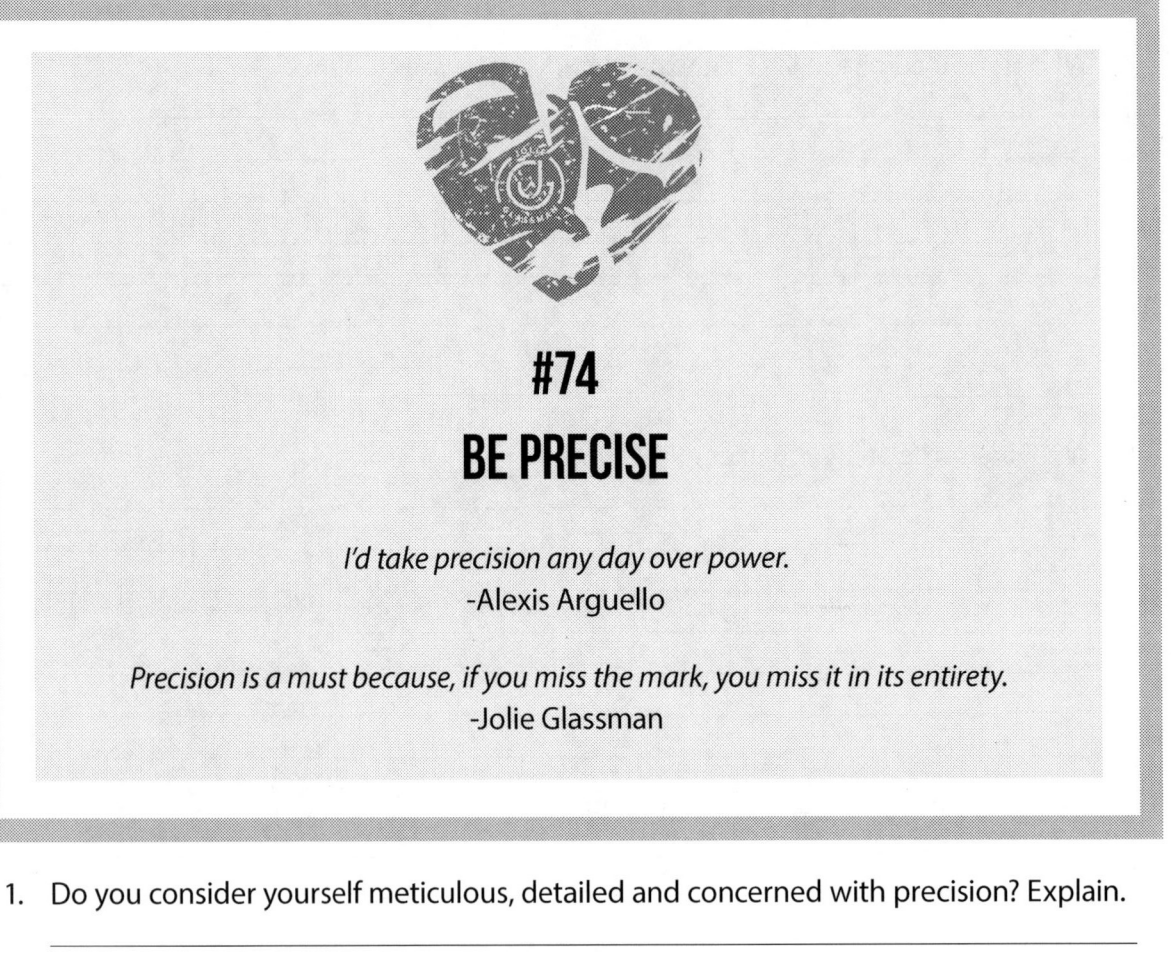

#74

BE PRECISE

I'd take precision any day over power.
-Alexis Arguello

Precision is a must because, if you miss the mark, you miss it in its entirety.
-Jolie Glassman

1. Do you consider yourself meticulous, detailed and concerned with precision? Explain.

_____
_____
_____
_____
_____
_____

2. What do you do in life where precision is very important?

_____
_____
_____
_____
_____
_____

3. Where in your life could more precision be added to become better?

_____
_____
_____
_____
_____
_____

4. What can you do to become more precise? Which skills and knowledge do you need to acquire?

_____

_____

_____

_____

_____

_____

5. Who do you admire in life that is very precise and therefore has excellent results?

_____

_____

_____

_____

_____

_____

6. Who do you need to be/become? Which qualities do you need to possess?

_____

_____

_____

_____

_____

7. What activities do you do daily that requires a lot of precision?

_____

_____

_____

_____

_____

8. What do you do specifically to ensure precision?

_____

_____

_____

_____

_____

9. What will you do to become more precise in the area(s) that need it?

_____

_____

_____

_____

_____

#75
EXPERIENCE MOSTLY WINS

*With experience in boxing, you learn how to be a
scientific boxer and how to fight easy.*
-Manny Paquiao

*You don't compare a guy with 30 or 40 fights with a guy
who had 200 fights and fought over 25 years.*
-Jake Lamotta

*We must pay our dues, lay the groundwork, and be consistent. If we want to
be known for something and excel at it, we need to work harder than anyone
else to stand out from the rest. Gain experience if you like winning.*
-Jolie Glassman

1. Which area in your life are you very experienced?

   _____
   _____
   _____
   _____

2. Why do you believe you are so experienced in this area?

   _____
   _____
   _____
   _____

3. Do you excel in that area and produce great results? Why or why not?

   _____
   _____
   _____

4. Who is more experienced than you in this area? Who are your role models in this area to keep learning from and gaining more experience?

_____

_____

_____

_____

_____

5. Which area in life do you need/want to gain more experience?

_____

_____

_____

_____

_____

6. What will you do to gain that experience and when will you start?

_____

_____

_____

_____

7. What have you done so far to gain/gather experience?

_____

_____

_____

_____

8. In the area you need/want more experience, what do the most experienced people possess that you need to have or learn more of?

_____

_____

_____

_____

9. What has been holding you back?

_____

_____

_____

_____

10. When can you move it out of the way? What will you do? By when?

_____

_____

_____

_____

#76

YOU WILL LEARN HOW STRONG YOU REALLY ARE

Impossible is just a big word thrown around by small men who find it easier to live in the world they've been given than to explore the power they have to change it. Impossible is not a fact. It's an opinion. Impossible is not a declaration. It's a DARE. Impossible is potential. Impossible is temporary. Impossible is nothing.
-Muhammad Ali

When you push yourself past your limits, fight through the storm, and refuse to give up no matter what, as your goal is more important than any excuses, you get to discover how very strong you really are. If you are not getting stronger, you are getting weaker, as nothing stays the same.
-Jolie Glassman

1. When was a time you proved to yourself that you could do something, yet it was a fight?
_____
_____
_____
_____

2. What was the process you went through?
_____
_____
_____

3. Which obstacles did you face?
_____
_____
_____

4. How did you overcome them?

5. Who did you need to be to overcome them?

6. What are daily things you do that show you are strong?

7. Which area in your life could use more strength?

8. What's missing?

9. What will you add and change? Who do you need to become?

10. What are things you can do and ways of being you can embody, when you need to be strong?

11. What are phrases and affirmations you can say to yourself to ensure strength is your only option?

#77

TEMPTATION IS A REAL THING

Temptation is the biggest drug in the world.
-Mike Tyson

Know what your temptations are and create boundaries beforehand
so that they will not trigger you or you will not give in to them.
-Jolie Glassman

1. What are things that tempt you? List as many as you can.

   _____
   _____
   _____
   _____
   _____

2. What are things and triggers that persuade you to give in to your temptations?

   _____
   _____
   _____
   _____

3. What is a *bad* habit you used to have/do, that you kicked and no longer do?

   _____
   _____
   _____
   _____

4. How did you kick the habit?

   _____
   _____
   _____

5. Who did you need to become?

_____

_____

_____

_____

6. What were winning phrases you said to yourself, to not cave into temptation?

_____

_____

_____

_____

7. What is your biggest temptation that you often give in to, while wishing you didn't?

_____

_____

_____

8. What happens?

_____

_____

_____

9. What happens just before you give into temptation?

_____

_____

_____

10. What could you do instead?

_____

_____

_____

11. How will you know to do this?

_____

_____

_____

12. When will you start?

_____

_____

_____

13. What will you create to eliminate triggers for this temptation?

_____

_____

_____

#78
DON'T SHOW WEAKNESSES

I'm scared every time I go in the ring, but it's how you handle it. What you have to do is plant your feet, bite down on your mouthpiece and say, 'Let's go'.
-Mike Tyson

You want to work on your strengths and show all your best to the world. Be strong and do what strong does. Practice what you need to, whatever you are weak in, but do not exploit yourself by showing what you are not good at, as people will remember what you show them.
-Jolie Glassman

1. What do you really do well?

_____

_____

_____

2. What about you, makes you do it well?

_____

_____

_____

3. Think of something you do well. Who are you being while doing it? Describe.

_____

_____

_____

4. What do you not do well? What are your weaknesses?

_____

_____

_____

5. Which strengths do you have that can override your weakness to make up for it?

_____

_____

_____

_____

6. Who do you hire or go to for support in areas you're not strong?

_____

_____

_____

7. Which area(s) are you weak in that you know you need to strengthen?

_____

_____

_____

8. How bad do you want to be stronger in this area?

_____

_____

_____

9. Who are you being while performing this activity?

_____

_____

_____

10. Who do you need to become to be stronger and strengthen it?

_____

_____

_____

11. What can you say to yourself and believe about yourself, to become stronger in this area?

_____

_____

_____

12. What can you do? Which skills do you need to acquire in order to grow stronger in this area?

_____

_____

_____

13. When will you start? What are your expectations for growth? What is your time frame?

_____

_____

_____

#79

PAIN AND SUFFERING
ARE PART OF IT

I hated every minute of training, but I said, 'Don't quit. Suffer now and live the rest of your life as a champion.'
-Muhammad Ali

Whatever has happened to you has also happened for you. The only way out is in; therefore, you need to go through the pain to get out of it. There is no going around it. Go through it, and grow through it, to the other side, which is joy, as what doesn't kill us makes us stronger.
-Jolie Glassman

1. **When was a time you suffered a lot of pain? Physically? Emotionally? Mentally?**

_____

_____

_____

_____

2. **How did you get through and handle it?**

_____

_____

_____

3. **Did you handle it in the most optimal way? Was it the way you wanted?**

_____

_____

_____

_____

4. How could you have handled it better?

_____

_____

_____

_____

5. When was a time you felt a lot of pain but didn't suffer, and you handled everything well?

_____

_____

_____

6. What did you do that prevented you from suffering? Who were you being?

_____

_____

_____

7. Do you have a high tolerance for pain?

_____

_____

_____

8. Why did you answer *yes* or *no*? Explain.

_____

_____

_____

9. What do you do, think, and feel to process and handle pain?

_____

_____

_____

10. How do you grieve?

_____

_____

_____

11. Do you deal with it effectively and *allow* yourself to go/grow through it?

_____

_____

_____

12. What could you do differently, take out, or put into place to help you deal with painful situations better?

_____

_____

_____

#80

HOW YOU TRAIN IS HOW YOU FIGHT

If you work hard in training, the fight is easy.
-Manny Paquiao

It's less about the physical training in the end, than it is about the mental preparation: boxing is a chess game. You have to be skilled enough, and have trained hard enough to know how many different ways you can counterattack in any situation, at any moment.
-Jimmy Smits

We cannot expect to win if we do not practice, study, and train to win. Know what you want and what it takes to get it. How you prepare will always translate to your performance. Champions are made when nobody is watching.
-Jolie Glassman

1. How do you prepare for fights, negotiations, projects, presentations, etc.?
   _____
   _____
   _____

2. Are you slow to start or slow to finish? What is your approach?
   _____
   _____
   _____

3. Where and when are you most powerful and energetic?
   _____
   _____
   _____

4. When do you often have low energy? Explain in detail.

_____

_____

_____

5. What are things you say to yourself when you're most powerful and energetic versus things you say to yourself when you have low energy?

_____

_____

_____

6. Which area of your life could use more training to get better results?

_____

_____

_____

7. What more can you do and add to improve?

_____

_____

_____

8. When are the best times and days to do this?

_____

_____

9. What are things you will say to yourself to get moving the quickest?

_____

_____

10. When will you start and how often will you do this?

_____

_____

11. When was a time you trained or prepared really hard for something, and you got great results?

_____

_____

12. Who were you being and what were you doing that was so great or intense, that got you those great results?

_____

_____

13. Are you being those ways and doing those things in the areas that need better results, and therefore better training? What is missing and by when will you add it?

_____

_____

#81
DON'T TAKE UNNECESSARY PUNISHMENT

*I took unnecessary punishment when I was fighting, Subconsciously - I
didn't know it then - I fought like I didn't deserve to live.*
-Jake La Motta

*Just because you can handle something doesn't mean you should take it, especially
unnecessarily. Avoid that which does not serve you as best as possible.*
-Jolie Glassman

1. We have all heard the saying *misery enjoys company*. Which bad habit(s) do you practice
   in life that while doing it, you then do more *bad* things and make it even worse?

   _____
   _____
   _____
   _____
   _____

2. Where in life are you making promises and commitments to yourself and not keeping
   them, therefore causing unnecessary punishment to yourself?

   _____
   _____
   _____
   _____
   _____

3. Where can your life improve?

   _____
   _____
   _____
   _____

4. What has been keeping you from excelling in this/these area(s)?

_____
_____
_____
_____
_____
_____
_____
_____
_____

5. How would you prefer to *be* and *feel* instead?

_____
_____
_____
_____
_____
_____
_____
_____
_____

6. What will you do to *be* and *feel* those ways?

_____
_____
_____
_____
_____
_____
_____
_____

7. What can you do in the future to get out of a funk the quickest when you are feeling down, disempowered, and negative?

_____
_____
_____
_____
_____
_____
_____
_____

#82

ROLL WITH THE PUNCHES

That's my gift. I let the negativity roll off me like water off a duck's back. If it's not positive, I didn't hear it. If you can overcome that, fights are easy.
-George Foreman

In life you want to be able to cope with challenges, withstand adversity, and let the wind help carry you. Do not go against it and get rocked by it. Where we resist, things persist. Take a step back and roll with it.
-Jolie Glassman

1. How does it look/feel like for you when you are *rolling with the punches*?

   _____
   _____
   _____

2. What are some of the circumstances, or scenarios, where you get confronted, stuck, and find it hard to *roll with the punches?*

   _____
   _____
   _____

3. What happens?

   _____
   _____

4. What are your thoughts during these situations?

   _____
   _____

5. What are the fears that arise?

   _____
   _____

6. Where do you feel it in your body and what happens?

    _____

    _____

    _____

7. How do you get out of these situations and solve them?

    _____

    _____

    _____

8. Who do you need to be?

    _____

    _____

    _____

9. What are some circumstances or scenarios, where you find it is easy to roll with the punches and handle what comes your way smoothly?

    _____

    _____

    _____

10. What happens?

    _____

    _____

    _____

11. What are your thoughts in these situations?

    _____

    _____

12. How do you feel?

    _____

    _____

13. How do you get out of these situations and solve them with the most ease?

    _____

    _____

14. Which skills do you possess that assist you with handling things smoothly and almost effortlessly?

    _____

    _____

15. Which area in life would you like to roll with the punches more? What can you do differently to ensure doing this? Who do you need to become to not get so reactive?

    _____

    _____

#83

FIGHT WHEN YOU DON'T WANT TO FIGHT

Don't quit. Suffer now and live the rest of your life as a champion.
-Muhammad Ali

Even if you think you cannot keep going, get ready to surprise yourself and show what you really can accomplish when do keep going and do not give up. We all already know what giving up feels like, and it is not rewarding. So suffer in the moment, yet reap the benefits for the longer term.
-Jolie Glassman

1. When was a time you kept fighting for something, even though you wanted to give up? What had you push through and keep fighting?

   _____
   _____
   _____
   _____
   _____

2. Which area of life do you need to try/fight harder to accomplish what you want to achieve?

   _____
   _____
   _____
   _____

3. What are you doing in that area now that is positive and helps push you forward?

   _____
   _____
   _____
   _____

4. What are you doing that holds you back from being even further along?

_____

_____

_____

_____

5. What can you put into place to ensure you will not give up, and you will push harder, and you will fight even when you do not want to?

_____

_____

_____

_____

_____

6. Who do you need to become? What do you need to believe about yourself?

_____

_____

_____

_____

_____

7. What needs to occur for you to get the hang of this?

_____

_____

_____

_____

8. Which new habits will you put in place?

_____

_____

_____

_____

9. How often and with what frequency?

_____

_____

_____

_____

10. When will you start?

_____

_____

_____

_____

#84

COME OUT WINNING

Boxers have to have the skill, and the will, but the will must be stronger than the skill.
-Muhammad Ali

In life, if you begin a winner and have a winning mindset,
you are already halfway there. Think, be, and act as if you
had already won, and live accordingly to achieve it.
Plan to win, think you are going to win, see the win, do what it
takes to win, taste the win and behave as the winner.
-Jolie Glassman

1. While going after something, do you doubt yourself or see yourself winning? Explain.

   _____
   _____
   _____
   _____
   _____
   _____
   _____

2. When was a time in life that you felt really positive about how the end results would go, you felt great, and you just knew you were going to win and then you did? Explain what happened.

   _____
   _____
   _____
   _____
   _____
   _____

3. When was a time in life that you felt the opposite, like you were not going to win in the endeavor you were after, and you were right and did not win? Explain what happened.

_____

_____

_____

_____

_____

_____

_____

_____

4. What did you do, and how did you feel, differently in the time you felt you were going to win and did win versus the time you felt you would not win and you were right?

_____

_____

_____

_____

_____

_____

_____

_____

5. What can you do and practice to ensure you have a winning mindset and believe you will win?

_____

_____

_____

_____

_____

_____

_____

6. Which phrases and affirmations can you say to yourself that will motivate you to begin with a winning mindset?

_____

_____

_____

_____

_____

_____

_____

_____

#85

DON'T UNDERESTIMATE YOUR OPPONENTS, AND DON'T OVERESTIMATE THEM EITHER

If you ever dream of beating me, you'd better wake up and apologize.
-Muhammad Ali

Assumption is the mother of the screw-up.
-Angelo Dundee

*The less you guesstimate, approximate, and assume, the better
off you will be, and the closer you will be to the desired target.
You will have fewer mistakes and more accuracy.*
-Jolie Glassman

1. Do you often overestimate your opponents, or underestimate them? Is it always one of them versus the other, or both? Explain your response.

   _____
   _____
   _____

2. How do you feel when you overestimate your opponent(s), and think they're better than they really are?

   _____
   _____
   _____

3. How does this affect you and your output?

   _____
   _____
   _____

4. In these scenarios, how are you left feeling about yourself?

_____

_____

_____

5. How do you feel when you underestimate your opponent(s), and think they're worse than they really are?

_____

_____

_____

6. How does this affect you and your output?

_____

_____

_____

7. In these scenarios, how are you left feeling about yourself?

_____

_____

_____

8. When was a time you either underestimated or overestimated an opponent and things did not work in your favor because of it?

_____

_____

_____

9. Was there a time it did work in your favor? Explain.

_____

_____

_____

10. How do you operate best?

_____

_____

_____

11. How do you best prepare for competition or to go up against an opponent?

_____

_____

_____

12. Which thoughts and behaviors do you exemplify when you are in a peak state, while not worrying about your opposition as you are on point?

_____

_____

#86
STAY ACTIVE, KEEP MOVING, NEVER STOP

*All fighters run. The constant motion prepares you for being
in the ring. And running strengthens your legs.
Punching power comes from your lower body.*
-Laila Ali

*In life, you want to stay in action, as learning what you do not want
to do is just as valuable as learning what you do want.*
-Jolie Glassman

1. Do you consider yourself an active person?

_____

_____

_____

_____

2. Why did you answer the way you did? What do you do, or not do?

_____

_____

_____

3. Would you like to become more active? In which ways? In which scenarios?

_____

_____

_____

4. Was there a time in life you were more active? When? How did you feel? What motivated you?

_____

_____

_____

5. Which activity do you engage in where you are active and constantly moving?

_____

_____

_____

6. How does that make you feel? What are your results like in this area?

_____

_____

_____

7. How active do you want to be, with what frequency, and how do you want to feel?

_____

_____

_____

8. What are some things you can do to become more active, things that interests you, and you feel would be enjoyable?

_____

_____

_____

9. Why aren't you doing those things now? What stops/prevents you?

_____

_____

_____

10. What are the consequences to your non-activity in certain areas?

_____

_____

_____

11. What will you add in your daily routine to encourage more activity?

_____

_____

_____

12. Which phrases, affirmations, mantras, or incantations can you say to motivate yourself to be/get active when you fall back?

_____

_____

_____

13. When will you start? How much time will you dedicate to this?

_____

_____

_____

#87

STUDY YOUR COMPETITION, OUTWIT YOUR OPPONENTS, AND CREATE LEVERAGE

If a guy beats me once, he'll have to do it again to make me believe him.
-Sugar Ray Leonard

In life, find where you have an advantage, and know that an advantage is only an advantage if you use it. Be a product of self-education. Study. Do things nobody else does and do them better.
-Jolie Glassman

1. Do you know your competition?

_____

_____

_____

_____

2. Who is your competition?

_____

_____

_____

3. What do you know about your competition?

_____

_____

_____

4. Which advantages do you feel you have over them?

_____

_____

_____

5. Do you know which advantages they have over you? What?

_____

_____

_____

6. What have you done, or can you do, to outwit your competition?

_____

_____

_____

7. How can you create leverage and come out on top?

_____

_____

_____

8. Do you consider yourself a person who wins at what you attempt and chase? Why?

_____

_____

_____

9. Is winning important to you? Why or why not?

_____

_____

_____

10. Why do you do the work that you do?

_____

_____

_____

11. What is your advantage and edge in the marketplace? What do you do better than anyone else?

_____

_____

_____

12. What can you add to raise the bar and outwit your competition?

_____

_____

13. Who do you need to be/become to rise-up and take the lead?

_____

_____

14. What actions can/will you take, by when, and with what frequency?

_____

_____

#88

BE PROUD OF YOURSELF — CELEBRATE YOUR WINS

I'm a winner each and every time I go into the ring.
-George Foreman

Celebrate when you accomplish things big or small. Get good at cheering for yourself and have a volume control for the voices in your head. Mute the voices that disempower you and raise the volume on those that inspire you.
-Jolie Glassman

1. Do you celebrate your wins?

    _____
    _____
    _____
    _____
    _____

2. What does celebrating your wins look like to you?

    _____
    _____
    _____
    _____
    _____

3. What are some wins that you celebrated, and what are some wins that you feel you missed out on celebrating?

    _____
    _____
    _____
    _____
    _____

4. How do you know you accomplished celebrating your wins?

_____
_____
_____
_____
_____
_____
_____
_____

5. Do you often go overboard celebrating, or do you focus on your next win and don't even acknowledge them? Explain.

_____
_____
_____
_____
_____
_____

6. How can you reward your wins in a healthy way that will also inspire you, and have you feel satisfied that you celebrated?

_____
_____
_____
_____
_____
_____

7. What is a challenge, and with what specific reward, can you take on that inspires you to complete it?

_____
_____
_____
_____
_____
_____

8. When will you start? What needs to be put into place? How long will it take to complete to get your reward?

_____
_____
_____
_____
_____
_____

#89

INSPIRE OTHERS TO BE GREAT - SERVE

*Success is attaining your dream while helping others
to benefit from that dream materializing.*
-Sugar Ray Leonard

Service to others is the rent you pay for a room here on Earth.
-Muhammad Ali

*The secret to living is giving. Use your life as a vehicle to serve.
I like to call it business in balance. Serve and contribute as an extension
of who you are and what you do, in all the roles you play.*
-Jolie Glassman

1. What does serving, and excellent service look like and mean to you?

_____

_____

_____

_____

2. Who do you admire most for their service in this world? List a few.

_____

_____

_____

_____

3. What do they do that is so great and impressive?

_____

_____

_____

_____

4. What do you possess in life that's so great and you can share with others?

_____

_____

_____

_____

_____

5. Where can you serve/contribute to make a difference?

_____

_____

_____

_____

_____

6. What are you currently doing that serves?

_____

_____

_____

_____

_____

7. How does it make you feel?

_____

_____

_____

_____

_____

8. What are you currently doing that you can share with others, inspire, and make a difference?

_____

_____

_____

_____

9. With which group of people? Be as specific as possible.

_____

_____

_____

_____

10. How will it look? When will you start?

_____

_____

_____

_____

#90

HIRE AND HAVE A COACH

Don't be afraid to employ people that will force you out of your comfort zone.
-George Foreman

People can do more than they ever believed they could do physically, emotionally, mentally, and academically when they have a coach. You have to be pushed, encouraged, developed, guided, and held accountable.
-Jolie Glassman

1. Do you currently have an accountability partner or a coach?

_____
_____
_____
_____

2. Have you ever had a coach? Why or why not?

_____
_____
_____
_____

3. Who were your favorite teachers? Why?

_____
_____
_____

4. Who pushes and holds you accountable to what you want/plan to create?

_____
_____
_____

5. Who do you aspire to be like and who are your role models?

_____

_____

_____

6. Do you surround yourself with people you aspire to be and admire? Why or why not?

_____

_____

_____

7. Which area of your life would you like to excel in where you currently do not as much as you would like?

_____

_____

_____

8. Have you considered hiring a coach/mentor?

_____

_____

_____

9. Do you believe you can make exponentially more money with a coach, and then the cost for the coach would be way worth it?

_____

_____

_____

10. What holds you back from hiring a coach?

_____

_____

_____

11. Are any of those things holding you back valid in exchange for the ROI you would get, if you had a coach?

_____

_____

_____

12. Can you move them out of the way to get the help/support you need?

_____

_____

13. If your life isn't working as well as you'd like it to in one or more areas, and you would like it to be/work better, when will you hire a coach and where will you find this person? Who will it be?

_____

_____

#91

SOMETIMES THE TOWEL NEEDS TO BE THROWN IN

*We all think we've got one more boxing match in us, and that, probably will
be the downfall of Floyd Mayweather, George Foreman, Manny Paquiao.
We'll overstay our welcome.*
-George Foreman

*Know when you are fighting a losing battle and get out while you
still can. Fight battles worth fighting for. Sometimes it
is more beneficial to quit what is not going to work out than
to carry on and get pummeled. Know the difference.*
-Jolie Glassman

1. Are you a person who pushes past their limits? Why?

   _____

   _____

   _____

2. Do you know when to hold 'em, know when to fold 'em, know when to walk away, and
   know when to run? Explain what you know about this.

   _____

   _____

   _____

3. Who do you turn to for an objective opinion? Who is your support system?

   _____

   _____

4. When was a time you worked so hard and knew things weren't going to get better and
   you just knew it was better to quit while behind and throw in the towel?

   _____

   _____

5. Is there an area of life where you feel you need to throw in the towel and create a new elsewhere?

_____

_____

_____

6. What can you take out that's not productive and conducive to progress, for yourself and your life? What can you add in its place that will be much better?

_____

_____

_____

7. How do you know when it's best to throw in the towel because you're behind versus just quitting for no optimal reasons?

_____

_____

_____

8. Do you often feel like giving up?

_____

_____

_____

9. In which predicaments or circumstances do you most feel like quitting?

_____

_____

10. Is there something in your life that you *should* quit because it does not serve you? What is it?

_____

_____

11. Why do you keep doing it and not quit?

_____

_____

12. What can you put into place, that would have you pivot to something more lucrative?

_____

_____

13. Is there an area of life where you find yourself quitting unnecessarily? What is it?

_____

_____

14. What can you do, and who can you be, to keep pushing forward and never give up?

_____

_____

#92
EVERY PUNCH SETS UP THE NEXT — GENERATE POWER

*It's like someone jammed an electric light bulb in your face and busted it.
I thought half my head was blowed off...When he knocked me down
I could have stayed there for three weeks.*
-James J Braddock

*Everything you do has an effect on everything else. If you do not do
something well, then the next item in the order will not be good either.*
-Jolie Glassman

1. What is something you did/do in life that required a lot of foundation?
_____
_____
_____

2. What are the stages and layers you needed to overcome to generate momentum and success?
_____
_____

3. What skills did you possess and then build upon to get positive results?
_____
_____

4. Which area of your life is not working so well?
_____
_____

5. What are you currently doing in that area?
_____
_____

6. What is missing that you can add in to make it work better?

_____

_____

7. Where are *weak links* in your life?

_____

_____

8. What can you do differently to not have *weak links*, and who would you need to be?

_____

_____

9. Which area of life are you strong and produce great results?

_____

_____

10. Who are you being in that area? What are you doing that is so special that has you produce such great results?

_____

_____

11. Where in life can you apply this to get greater results?

_____

_____

12. Where do you lose momentum?

_____

_____

13. What happens when you lose momentum? Do you start again or give up? If you start again, how does that happen?

_____

_____

14. What's missing for you to keep it going and not lose momentum?

_____

_____

15. Which new skills do you need to gain?

_____

_____

16. Who do you admire that possesses these skills?

_____

_____

17. What about them do you admire? How can you incorporate this way of being into your daily life and embody it?

_____

_____

#93

CONTROL YOUR BREATHING: SELF-REGULATE

You know if you want to be a boxer the first time you get hit on the nose.
-Ricky Hatton

The more oxygen you take in, and the deeper and fuller you breathe, the better. Breathe as if you have a large nose on your chest and heart, and inhale through your heart center, fully and deeply.
-Jolie Glassman

1. Do you currently have a breathwork practice? Explain.

    _____
    _____
    _____
    _____
    _____
    _____

2. Are you aware of your breathing? Do you use breathing to self-regulate?

    _____
    _____
    _____
    _____
    _____

3. Do you have anxiety, tiredness, stress or lack of focus in any areas? Where?

    _____
    _____
    _____
    _____
    _____

4. What causes this for you?

_____
_____
_____
_____
_____
_____

5. Describe your breathing in these areas/scenarios?

_____
_____
_____
_____
_____
_____

6. Can you add a breathing practice to self-regulate when these scenarios occur? Explain.

_____
_____
_____
_____
_____

7. What daily activities do you do where you feel completely in the zone?

_____
_____
_____
_____
_____

8. Who are you being?

_____
_____
_____
_____
_____

9. What are some activities you can add into life that fulfill you, and have you in these coherent zones?

_____
_____
_____
_____
_____

#94

ALWAYS BE IN SHAPE AND SUPER FIT AND LEAN

I run, but boxing conditioning is different, so you have to get used to running in the ring. Boxing movements are very different. I train very hard at things that mimic boxing. I have to do mostly sport-specific training, such as lots of sparring.
-Wladimir Klitschko

Generally, the more weight you put on, the less effective you are.
-Sugar Ray Leonard

I have always adhered to two principles. The first one is to train hard and get in the best physical condition. The second is to forget about the other fellow until you face him in the ring and the bell sounds for the fight.
-Rocky Marciano

Stay in shape so you do not have to keep getting into shape. When you start taking care of yourself, you start feeling better, you start looking better, and you start to attract better. It all starts within you. Prevention is easier than correction. Make being fit a must, not a should, and you will always be fit and in shape.
-Jolie Glassman

1. Do you consider yourself to be in shape, super fit, and lean?

_____

_____

_____

2. How long have you been this way?

_____

_____

_____

3. Was there ever a time in your life you were in shape, super fit, and lean?

_____

_____

_____

4. When? What were you doing? How often? Why did you stop?

_____

_____

_____

5. Is it important for you to be in shape, super fit and lean? Why?

_____

_____

_____

6. What do you do daily to ensure you are in shape, super fit and lean?

_____

_____

_____

7. What do you do daily that does _not_ align with being in shape and fit?

_____

_____

_____

8. What are you willing to put in, that if you added, could make all the difference?

_____

_____

_____

9. What are you willing to take out or stop doing/eating, that could make all the difference?

_____

_____

10. How do you feel when you are in shape and super fit? How do you feel when you are not?

_____

_____

11. What happens that pulls you out of the game/routine and how do you generate yourself to get back into the game of getting in shape and fit?

_____

_____

12. What will it take for you to be consistent for life? Who do you need to become? What do you need to believe to ensure you will stick to being in shape and super fit for life?

_____

_____

_____

#95
THERE ARE NO SHORTCUTS TO SUCCESS

I've found that taking shortcuts will get you to the place you don't want to be much quicker than they get you to the place you want to be.
-Lennox Lewis

Those who are at the top struggled and fought their way there, one step at a time, just like all the others. Life is a journey. Take it step by step. It is a process, so enjoy the journey.
-Jolie Glassman

1. Which area of your life, or something you have done, where you worked super hard to achieve for a long time?

   _____
   _____
   _____

2. Which skills and personality traits did you possess and display to accomplish this great feat?

   _____
   _____

3. How do you feel when you work hard to accomplish something versus when you do not?

   _____
   _____

4. Where in life do you cut corners and try to take shortcuts?

   _____
   _____

5. How does that play out for you?

   _____
   _____

6. Where in life do you need to give more effort and not cut corners?

_____

_____

7. What is missing that would have you grinding and pushing through?

_____

_____

8. Which other skills do you need to gain/acquire to follow through and not cut yourself short?

_____

_____

9. What is something you have been wanting to do or accomplish, but you don't because it will take too much time?

_____

_____

10. When will you begin?

_____

_____

11. Have you ever succeeded very easily at something? What?

_____

_____

12. Why do you think it was so easy for you?

_____

_____

13. Which kind of results have you witnessed that impress you?

_____

_____

14. Does hard work scare you, or not interest you?

_____

_____

15. What is something you are willing to add into your life to encourage hard and consistent work?

_____

_____

16. Who do you need to be/become? Which characteristics and behaviors can you add?

_____

_____

17. What can you put into place when you want to quit, yet, also want to be successful? Which systems can you put into place to ensure this will happen when needed?

_____

_____

#96

RECOVERY IS A DAILY MUST

An injury is not just a process of recovery, it is also a process of discovery.
-Conor McGregor

I always say, 'The moments between the notes create the music.' The in-between is very important and needed for the process and the whole. What we surrender to, we allow. We must create space in the body. We must learn to relax and chill out and to recover and heal daily, and all of that occurs only during rest.
-Jolie Glassman

1. Do you love yourself? Why or why not?

    _____
    _____
    _____
    _____
    _____

2. How do you prove and show you love yourself?

    _____
    _____
    _____
    _____
    _____

3. Is recovery part of your daily routine?

    _____
    _____
    _____
    _____
    _____

4. What does your recovery routine(s) look like?

_____
_____
_____
_____
_____

5. Are you rested and recovered on a daily basis?

_____
_____
_____
_____
_____

6. Do you know how to relax?

_____
_____
_____
_____
_____

7. What does *relaxing* look like to you?

_____
_____
_____
_____
_____

8. What do you do that burns you out daily?

_____
_____
_____
_____

9. Are you good at surrendering?

_____
_____
_____
_____

10. Why are you good at it or not?

_____
_____
_____
_____

11. Do you have any pain or injuries? Where in your body and when does it mostly occur?

_____
_____
_____
_____
_____
_____

12. Do you work on healing and recovering on your own? In which ways?

_____
_____
_____
_____
_____
_____

13. Do you believe you can heal yourself? Explain why you believe the way you do.

_____
_____
_____
_____
_____
_____

14. What needs to happen and occur for you to begin the recovery process yourself?

_____
_____
_____
_____
_____

15. Which skills and knowledge do you need to acquire?

_____
_____
_____
_____
_____

16. Who do you follow and learn from, in order to know how to recover?

_____
_____
_____
_____
_____

17. Do you meditate daily and/or practice breathwork and self-regulation? If not, do you plan to learn and practice?

_____

_____

_____

_____

_____

_____

18. Do you want to have a daily practice? Why or why not? Explain.

_____

_____

_____

_____

_____

_____

19. What are some things you do to unwind and recover?

_____

_____

_____

_____

_____

20. What can you do to recover and feel better to get out of pain?

_____

_____

_____

_____

_____

21. What are some things you would like to add to your daily routine to assist in healing and recovery?

_____

_____

_____

_____

_____

22. When will you add these things? With what frequency?

_____

_____

_____

_____

_____

#97

HEALTH AND DIET ARE OF TOP PRIORITY

You have to fight for your health and stay on top of it.
Our bodies are meant to be healthy.
-Laila Ali

Everything you do and eat contributes to the person you're becoming.
Prevention is much easier than correction. I am a believer in a whole-
language, whole-life approach. You need to read it, live it, see it, believe it,
talk about it, be about it, learn about it, and immerse yourself in it fully.
-Jolie Glassman

1. Which area of life, or in your health/wellness/body, do you want to transform?
   _____
   _____
   _____

2. Do you value your health and diet as a top priority? Why or why not?
   _____
   _____
   _____

3. Do you work on your health and strength daily? Explain what this looks like.
   _____
   _____
   _____

4. Where can you be healthier and stronger?
   _____
   _____
   _____

5. What can you do every day to make yourself healthier and stronger?

_____

_____

_____

_____

6. What can you add to your life and do daily, to make you better and faster?

_____

_____

_____

7. How is your diet? Describe it.

_____

_____

_____

8. What is not good about your diet and health habits?

_____

_____

_____

9. What can you change?

_____

_____

_____

10. How will you do it?

_____

_____

_____

11. Why now?

_____

_____

_____

12. Why not now?

_____

_____

_____

13. How healthy do you want to be? What will your lifestyle look like to be this way? Always ask yourself, *Does this contribute to being a healthy and fit person?*

_____

_____

_____

#98

TAKE RESPONSIBILITY

You can teach better by setting examples, than we do
by explaining and talking about them.
-Cus D'Amato

Elevate your life by taking responsibility for who you are. Become
conscious. You are here to create your own music, not someone else's.
Do not die with your music still in you. The road to power is taking
responsibility for your life, your success, your happiness, choices, and
your mind. Responsibility means being able to respond, not being
the effect of something but being able to affect something.
-Jolie Glassman

1. Are you a person who takes responsibility for everything that shows up for yourself and your life? Why or why not? Explain.

   _____
   _____
   _____
   _____
   _____
   _____

2. Are you blaming other people for your problems? Who? Explain.

   _____
   _____
   _____
   _____
   _____
   _____

3. How does faulting others make you feel?

_____

_____

_____

_____

_____

_____

4. How can you take control, accept responsibility, and work toward finding a solution?

_____

_____

_____

_____

_____

_____

5. Where in life do you need to take responsibility where you have not been?

_____

_____

_____

_____

_____

_____

6. Where, and how, can you *affect* change?

_____

_____

_____

_____

_____

7. What area(s) of your life would you like to change?

_____

_____

_____

_____

_____

8. What can you do next to take you in the direction of having it your way?

_____

_____

_____

_____

_____

#99

FINISH STRONG

*Only a man who knows what it is like to be defeated can reach
down to the bottom of his soul and come up with the extra
ounce of power it takes to win when the match is even.*
-Muhammad Ali

*Life is not about what happens. It is about how you react to what happens.
So it is not about the setbacks; it is about the comebacks.
Always make sure to finish fully and finish strong.*
-Jolie Glassman

1. When things get tough do you push through or quit?

_____
_____
_____
_____
_____

2. Why are you this way?

_____
_____
_____
_____
_____

3. Who do you need to become in order to finish strong?

_____
_____
_____
_____

4. Do you consider yourself a competitive person? Explain.

_____

_____

_____

_____

_____

5. Do you consider yourself a results producer? If not, do you want to be?

_____

_____

_____

_____

_____

6. Which area of life would you like to be stronger?

_____

_____

_____

_____

_____

7. What can you do to accomplish this?

_____

_____

_____

_____

_____

8. Who do you need to be/become?

_____

_____

_____

_____

9. What new thoughts and behaviors will you add to ensure you finish strong?

_____

_____

_____

_____

10. Are you a person that finishes strong?

_____

_____

_____

_____

11. Give some examples of when you finished strong and produced great, desirable results?

_____

_____

_____

_____

_____

_____

12. When did you want to give up, yet didn't? What did you do? What did you say to yourself, to push through and finish?

_____

_____

_____

_____

_____

_____

_____

13. Do you start things and then quit? Why or why not?

_____

_____

_____

_____

_____

14. Do you chase your dreams and fulfill upon your goals? Why or why not?

_____

_____

_____

_____

_____

15. Do you consider yourself a go-getter, or lazy? Explain.

_____

_____

_____

_____

_____

16. Where in life do you need to become more of a go-getter?

_____

_____

_____

_____

_____

17. What could you do, and who do you need to be, to become more of a go-getter? What skills do you need to acquire to push through things and circumstances and see them out to fruition?

_____
_____
_____
_____
_____
_____

18. When is your energy usually at its highest? When beginning endeavors, while pursuing them, or once achieving them?

_____
_____
_____
_____
_____
_____

19. When is your energy at its lowest?

_____
_____
_____
_____
_____
_____

20. What causes it to be high? What happens when you fizz out, get lazy, and lose your mojo?

_____
_____
_____
_____
_____
_____

21. Do you consider yourself a person that lives a passion filled life? Why or why not? What's missing?

_____
_____
_____
_____
_____
_____

#100
BE REFLECTIVE - EVALUATE

I don't believe in losses; I believe in lessons.
-Alicia Napoleon

The quality of your life is directly correlated to the quality of questions you ask yourself. Being reflective and evaluating is accomplished through strategic questioning. Everything hinges on the asking, the questions we ask ourselves and others. The answers are always in the questions. If we do not like the answers, we need to ask better questions. Change your questions and change your life.
-Jolie Glassman

1. Do you reflect daily?

2. What does that look like for you?

3. Do you reflect on most things you do? Why or why not?

4. What kind of information do you come up with while reflecting?

_____

_____

_____

_____

_____

5. Where and when can you be more reflective?

_____

_____

_____

_____

6. Do you journal daily? If so, what are the benefits you find? If not, why?

_____

_____

_____

_____

7. Do you find that you reflect and evaluate how things went? If it all went the way you wanted? How you could do it differently in the future?

_____

_____

_____

_____

8. Do you learn from past experiences and avoid repeating the same mistakes, or do you seem to repeat the same mistakes over and over again? Explain.

_____

_____

_____

_____

9. Are you pragmatic? Do you do what works and makes sense for you? Do you abstain from what doesn't work/make sense to you? Explain.

_____

_____

_____

_____

10. What are vices that you wish you didn't have?

_____

_____

_____

_____

11. What has kept them around and do you plan on giving them up? If so, when?

_____

_____

_____

_____

_____

12. Do you interject with your inner voice and make sure to ask better questions to get the most desirable results? Give some examples.

_____

_____

_____

_____

_____

13. What kinds of questions do you ask yourself on a daily basis? Think! In the mornings, afternoons, evenings? Notice the questions you often ask yourself. Do they serve you?

_____

_____

_____

_____

_____

14. Which questions do you often ask yourself that do not serve you? What are some better questions to intervene with and bring your vibration higher and get better answers to then deliver better results?

_____

_____

_____

_____

_____

15. Do you have clarity in your life and all that you are after achieving? Explain.

_____

_____

_____

_____

_____

16. How has life been going so far? Look back on all your years. Are you satisfied with where you are, who you are, all you have done and seen? Explain.

_____

_____

_____

_____

17. Do you have any regrets? If so, what are they? Can you do these things now?

_____

_____

_____

_____

18. What can you begin to do to prevent future regrets?

_____

_____

_____

_____

19. Who do you need to be/become?

_____

_____

_____

_____

20. If you could do things differently, what would you do and in which situations?

_____

_____

_____

_____

21. What makes you most proud of yourself?

_____

_____

_____

_____

22. What are your favorite qualities about yourself?

_____

_____

_____

_____

23. What are things you want to improve? What are things you will do to get better?

_____

_____

_____

_____

24. What are some of the things you learned in this book?

_____

_____

_____

25. What are some things you will apply in your life from this book?

_____

_____

_____

_____

26. What makes you a champion and what does not?

_____

_____

_____

_____

27. Who is your future self? Describe this person, 5 and 10 years from now. *Be Your Future Self Now.*

_____

_____

_____

_____

Questions to ask yourself.........

28. Who must I become to get to the next level?

_____

_____

_____

_____

29. What do I stand for?

_____

_____

_____

_____

30. What am I committed to.... (Being? Having? Doing?)?

_____

_____

_____

_____

31. What is my mission?

_____

_____

_____

32. Who am I?

33. What do I do best?

34. What do I love the most?

35. What actions align with that?

36. What am I already doing now that aligns with all my commitments?

37. Which actions am I doing now that I need to get rid of and stop doing?

38. What needs to be in its place?

39. What is my next best move?

#101

LEAVE A LEGACY

I want people to say that I fought for my rights. I fought for my people. I'm the most famous black man in the world. I'm a strong believer in God. If I die, I'm a legend.
-Muhammad Ali

You want to leave something; you really do. I mean, in the end, statues and all those things, that doesn't mean anything. Leave something we're all going to benefit from. I think that's what I'd like to do.
-George Foreman

People who do not find their greatness are irrelevant. Think of the reputation you want to build, your top passions and strengths, and the group of people you most want to serve, and then build it with consistent consistency.
-Jolie Glassman

1. Who do you want to be known for/as? After you leave this Earth, what would you like people to remember you for and say about you? Be specific.

    _____

    _____

    _____

    _____

2. What have you done to support that thus far?

    _____

    _____

    _____

    _____

3. What do you plan to do/add to reinforce that?

_____
_____
_____
_____
_____

4. Who do you admire, and what about them do you admire so much?

_____
_____
_____
_____
_____

5. Which qualities do you need to possess to become the person you want to be?

_____
_____
_____
_____
_____

6. Which qualities do you currently have that contribute to this manifestation?

_____
_____
_____
_____
_____

7. Which qualities do you need to become the greatest version of your future self?

_____
_____
_____
_____

8. Who do you need to be, to become your future self now? When are you starting?

_____
_____
_____
_____

9. What new actions, plans, and decisions will you make? By when?

_____
_____
_____
_____

CONCLUSION

Wherever you go, there you are. If you don't like your results, or life, change it. Like a boxer, make adversity work for you. You are the boss of you. You are the responsible party for your life. Take responsibility for everything that shows up for yourself and your life. Then you know you have the power, and you are able to respond. Become a master of your destiny, and not a victim of your history. Be the champion of your own life. Be the hero you have always been waiting for; be your future self now. You have what it takes and all you need is inside of you. It is never a lack of resources; it is a lack of resourcefulness. Be resourceful. Be grateful. Trade your expectations for appreciation and your whole life will change. You are who you practice being. Practice who you want to be and you will excel. Ask insightful questions to get great answers. However, when your answers are not optimal, ask better questions. Challenge yourself. Prove to yourself you can be more amazing than you ever even imagined. Show yourself how great you are. Perform. Shine. Strive. Never give up. You got this!

I learn so I can teach,

I share so I can transform,

I serve so I can live in joy.

I always say/feel, *I've been getting qualified my whole life and I've been called to serve. God doesn't call the qualified, he qualifies the called.* Thank you for allowing me to serve and contribute. Now go live an extraordinary life and be fearless in the pursuit of what sets your soul on fire. Be the boxing champion of your own life.

BONUSES

NO EXCUSES – FITNESS FOR LIFE
LIVE A LIFE OF HEALTH – FITNESS IS EVERYDAY

CREATE YOUR OWN WORKOUTS
CAN BE DONE AT HOME WITH LITTLE OR NO EQUIPMENT!

"Work harder on yourself, than you do on anything else, and life becomes easier."

Step 1: Decide total workout time.
Step 2: Choose what body parts to work out and choose exercises.
Step 3: Choose equipment needed & how many rounds and reps to fill the time allotted.
Step 4: Always do 5-15 min warm up/cool down

EQUIPMENT (if needed)
Timer
Jump Rope
Dumbbells (3, 5, 10 lb)
Resistance Bands / Loops
Foam Roller

TIME AND REPETITION EXAMPLES

5 - 10 Minutes: Choose 2 -10 exercises from list and do one every minute for a minute. (You may repeat exercise).

20 Minutes: Choose 10 exercises from list and do one every minute for a minute. Rest for 1 minute, repeat after 10 minutes.

40 Minutes - 1 hour: Choose 5 - 10 exercises and do rounds of 8-20 repetitions each or as many rounds as possible. Resting 1 minute between rounds.

WARM UP
Dynamic Stretching & Foam Rolling
(Movement / Warm Up)

COOL DOWN
Static Stretching & Foam Rolling

EXERCISES TO CHOOSE FROM

(choose from 2 to 10)

* print sheet and check off the ones you will do.

__ Squats
__ Lunges (front, back, side or static)
__ Burpees
__ Mountain Climbers
__ Plank Jacks
__ Shadow Boxing
__ Jumping Jacks
__ Curtsy Lunges
__ Squat Jumps
__ Bicep Curls
__ Tricep Kickbacks
__ Shoulder Press
__ Squat - Curl - Press
__ Squat - Push - Kick
__ High Knees
__ Butt Kickers
__ Jumping Rope
__ Manmakers
__ Push- Ups
__ 400M Run (1x around block)
__ Run Up/ Down Stairs
__ Run Specified # of Laps

@jolieglassman   jolieglassman.com

"DON'T GET IN SHAPE LIVE IN SHAPE!"

RECOVERY (ACTIVE / NON-ACTIVE)
& REST ARE ALL PART OF THE PROGRAM

AS HARD AS YOU WORKOUT:
THAT'S HOW HARD TO RECOVER
BALANCE!

SET YOURSELF UP TO SUCCEED (NOT TO FAIL)

1. Create ranges for yourself: (NEVER workout under 2 days a week & no need to go over 5, and don't skip more than 2 days in a row) 1 day turns into another – turns into another – turns into another... Consistency is key! Fitness is a daily activity.. for LIFE!

2. Whether you workout or not – you will have no time – SO WORKOUT! Nobody is too busy, it's just a matter or priorities. Health is KEY / Creating good habits is KEY. Selfcare is your Healthcare.
Fall in love with taking the best care of yourself.

3. Never the same rhythm, timing or tempo. You can do the same workout in a variety of ways. Just mix up the timing, speed, # of repetitions, order and tempo.
It's the moments between the notes that create the music.

4. You are the BOSS of you! You Choose! In every moment you are choosing - whether you recognize it or not. Think wisely. Honor yourself. Choose wiseley. Be empowered.

5. You are YOUR greatest investment. Invest fully in yourself. Self care is your superpower.
Utilize it! Listen to your body. - It's your best free coach.

6. Chase strong / Be strong. If you are not getting stronger you are getting weaker.
Nothing stays the same.

Top 3 Nutrition Tips!

■ Practice Intermittent Fasting. The more restricted the eating window the better.

■ Stay away from processed foods, ingredients you don't know, gluten, dairy & wheat. Eat a Whole Foods diet with mainly just that one ingredient of the food itself.

■ Drink at least 1 gallon of water throughout the day and begin right when you wake up with a 32oz glass of warm water with lemon.

@jolieglassman   jolieglassman.com

216

AFFIRMATIONS, MANTRAS & INCANTATIONS

Choose one and repeat it throughout the day. Harness their potential to help you stay on track, reach your goals, and find inner peace. So grab hold, take a deep breath, and fill yourself with motivation to power through each moment today.

* LOVE - LOVE - LOVE

* Be still and know.

* I am that, I am.

* God is my joy, love, and peace.

* How may I serve?

* I honor myself most when I'm alone.

* I am perfect, whole, and complete just as I am.

* I am beautiful as I am.

* I am enough.

* I have phenomenal coping skills.

* The world is a better place because I'm in it.

* Everything is always working out for me (because it is, it has, and it will continue to be).

* Everything is about having the right people in the right places supporting you.

* What is this situation here to teach or show me?

* Inner stillness is the key to inner strength.

* I am healthy, vibrant, and lean. I love and take care of myself.

* Say in the mirror: *"My body now restores itself to its natural state of health."*

* I love you very much (*insert your name here*) - you are perfect exactly the way you are.

* Go hero go!

* I have everything I need inside of me.

* It's perfect where I'm at and there's nowhere to get to.

* I am deeply thankful for the joy, abundance, and love that surrounds me every day.

* I have all the time in the world! What I choose to do every day supports my business, relationships, and personal growth exponentially. I am grateful, abundant, and present to receive the gift that I am blessed with all the time in the world. (thanks, April Love)

* I know the right person will be arriving in divine order at precisely the perfect time.

* Making money is easy for me.

* I am abundant, blessed, and grateful.

* The greater my success, the greater my ability to serve others.

* I am always at the right place, at the right time.

* I have all the time in the world.

* Life is happening for me, not to me.

* I always achieve my goals.

* I am directed, protected, and guided.

* I am love. I emanate from pure love. I am always connected to this source of love.

* I am a money magnet and money just flows to me.

* In gratitude, if I didn't do _____, this would've never happened. I am always exactly where I need to be.

* I am financially independent and earn at least (make up your own amount) per month.

* Infinite spirit, reveal to me the way. Let me know if there is anything for me to do. I am listening.

* Large sums of money come to me gracefully in perfect ways.

* Infinite spirit, open the way for my immediate supply. Let all that is mine by divine right now reach me in great avalanches of abundance, and please give me a sign, and let me know if there is anything for me to do.

* My heart is full with inspiration, gratitude, and kindness wherever I am!

* Wherever you go, there you are!

* Divine energy flows in me, flows through me, and is all around me.

* Every day, and in every way, I'm getting better and better.

* I do what I have to do 'til I can do what I want to do.

* Waking up this morning I smile. Twenty-four brand new hours are before me... Today I vow to live fully in each moment and to look at all beings with eyes of compassion.

Printed in the United States
by Baker & Taylor Publisher Services